Achieving Teaching Excellence

Achieving Teaching Excellence

Developing Your TEF Profile and Beyond

by
Peter Wolstencroft, Leanne de Main and
Paul Cashian
with a foreword by Professor Sally Brown

 Open University Press

Open University Press
McGraw-Hill Education
8th Floor, 338 Euston Road
London
England
NW1 3BH

email: enquiries@openup.co.uk
world wide web: www.openup.co.uk

and Two Penn Plaza, New York, NY 10121-2289, USA

First edition published 2021

A catalogue record of this book is available from the British Library

ISBN-13: 9780335249299
ISBN-10: 0335249299
eISBN: 9780335249305

Library of Congress Cataloging-in-Publication Data
CIP data applied for

Typeset by Transforma Pvt. Ltd., Chennai, India

Contents

Case Studies

The potential impact of the case studies on the main categories of the National Student Survey (NSS) is detailed below:

	The Teaching on my Course	Learning Opportunities	Assessment and Feedback	Academic Support	Organisation and Management	Learning Resources	Learning Community	Student Voice
1.1 Overcoming barriers in the teaching of mathematics	✔	✔						
1.2 Managing student expectations at a 'red brick' university	✔						✔	✔
3.1 Encouraging new approaches		✔				✔		
3.2 Supporting students in a time of crisis				✔			✔	✔
4.1 The TEF in Further Education	✔		✔					
4.2 COVID-19 – a forced change	✔			✔	✔	✔		
5.1 Disruptive Media Learning Lab		✔				✔		
5.2 WISEflow – a university-wide digital assessment platform			✔					
6.1 Students volunteering and some unintended consequences		✔					✔	
6.2 Responsible Futures							✔	
7.1 Further Education to Higher Education – you CAN do it!		✔			✔			✔
7.2 Strategies to reduce BAME attainment gap in Business Education				✔	✔		✔	✔

Foreword

There is a growing recognition worldwide of the importance of offering training, support and engagement throughout the careers of all those teaching and supporting learning in post-compulsory education, from initial entry to the profession through to continuous professional development (CPD) for the experienced old hands, who are keen to maintain currency. This comprehensive and research-informed book offers a panoply of ideas for colleagues to use practically in their teaching and learning practice. Particular strengths of the book include the use in each chapter of illustrative case studies including examples of pedagogic innovation, together with reflection prompts in the form of *Key Takeaways* summarising the crucial learning points of reflection, together with suggestions for readers on how to take the ideas therein and apply them in their own practice.

Each chapter takes a key theme of high relevance to the current learning context, offering very apposite guidance in a world in which the COVID-19 crisis has made every Further Education and Higher Education provider rethink the balance between face-to-face and virtual provision. They start with a discussion, good teaching practice and, in particular, an insistence that pedagogy must drive learning. Throughout this volume, the authors reinforce the importance of inclusive practice, wherein inequality of access to technologies is monitored and mitigated as far as possible, while at the same time illustrating the powerful benefits of technologies in supporting novel teaching approaches, including gaming and simulation which have served the community so well during the interruptions of 2020. The chapter on observation and the power of the group provides food for thought on how we can make these practices a fully developmental process.

Another key section covers the crucial topic of assessment, with chapters exploring how assessment can be a vehicle for learning as well as a means of recognising and accrediting it, as well as a discussion of how students working in partnership with curriculum deliverers and assessors can co-create knowledge in ways that are fit-for-purpose in the twenty-first century. Central to this approach is the use of feedback and feedforward to foreground such dialogic approaches, building on the *Assessment for Learning* movement that has underpinned advances in assessment in the last three decades.

Many academics nowadays concern themselves with how they can pre-empt inappropriate academic conduct, including cheating and plagiarism, which the authors argue involves designing authentic assessment to 'beat the cheats', as case study author Judith Darnell argues, which often makes for better pedagogic practice than assessment approaches that rely on traditional forms of assessment like unseen time-constrained exams and submitted coursework.

At a time when governments often insist that the key purpose of post-compulsory education is all about advancement and professional reward for graduates, this book instead argues for ensuring that Higher Education Institutes and college-based learning helps students to advance their employability through engaging with the outside world in a variety of formats.

Towards the end of the volume, the authors direct readers' thinking to ways in which practitioners can ensure that the student experience is enhanced by ensuring that research and teaching work symbiotically rather than in conflict with one another, with research feeding teaching practice and vice versa. This leads into an invaluable discussion of how diverse recent approaches to curriculum design and delivery can be used in the service of student learning.

This well-referenced and thought-provoking book will make a useful addition to the bookshelves of anyone in Further or Higher Education who is interested in advancing pedagogy and fostering student learning: I recommend it wholeheartedly to you.

Professor Sally Brown *is an Independent Consultant in Learning, Teaching and Assessment and Emerita Professor at Leeds Beckett University where she was, until 2010, Pro-Vice-Chancellor. She is also Visiting Professor at Edge Hill University and formerly at the Universities of Plymouth, Robert Gordon, South Wales and Liverpool John Moores and at universities in Australia – James Cook Central Queensland and the Sunshine Coast.*

She holds Honorary Doctorates from the Universities of Plymouth, Kingston, Bournemouth, Edinburgh Napier and Lincoln.

She is a Principal Fellow of the Higher Education Academy, a Staff and Educational Development Association (SEDA) Senior Fellow and a National Teaching Fellow.

Preface

Despite the desire of the 1992 Further and Higher Education Act to introduce a market to education and to free it from central regulation, the years since then have seen an increase in both directives from government and measurement in the sector. In 2018, as a result of the Higher Education and Research Act (HERA), the Office for Students (OfS) was established as the regulatory body for Higher Education in England. The four main areas of regulation state that students: are supported to access and succeed in Higher Education; receive a high-quality academic experience; are able to progress to employment or further study; and receive value for money. Both value for money and employability tend to be collected under the term 'the student experience' and it is around this that much of this book is centred. There have been many attempts to define and then codify these terms and whilst there is some disagreement about the definitions, the two surveys, introduced below, are used to measure organisations and become a key focus within education.

The Teaching Excellence Framework (commonly known as the TEF) was introduced in 2018 to measure both teaching excellence in universities and colleges, and how well they ensure positive outcomes for students in terms of further study and graduate-level employment. Organisations that participated were awarded ratings (Gold, Silver, Bronze or provisional) according to a range of metrics. Those providers who achieved a Gold rating (28% of providers at the time of writing) often use this as part of their marketing campaign, seeing it as confirmation of excellence, whilst all who participate are able to charge increased tuition fees. The TEF sources data from three key metrics to measure the performance of providers.

- Student satisfaction – National Student Survey (NSS)
- Continuation – Higher Education Statistics Agency (HESA)
- Employment outcomes – The Graduate Outcomes survey, previously known as Destination of Leavers from Higher Education (DLHE)

This book is subdivided into the three aspects of quality within education as defined by the TEF, namely, teaching quality, learning environment, and student outcome and learning gain. Our aim is to look at each aspect, highlight excellent practice from throughout the sector, and identify possible ways in which organisations can integrate innovation into their teaching and learning strategies.

One of the key metrics that is used in the TEF, the NSS, was originally launched in 2005, and is now seen as the key indicator of the student experience within education and its results are available to prospective applicants. The NSS is split into eight categories of questions and covers aspects such as teaching, assessment and the learning community. The key question for providers is question 27 (using the 2020 survey as our base), which reads as follows: 'Overall, I am satisfied with the quality of my course'. This is the question that is used as the headline figure for the providers and hence, is the one that is focused most upon. Although it is not the intention of this book to look at the various approaches that providers take in order to raise awareness and also to raise the overall score of the NSS, it is clear that organisations that perform well are those that embrace innovation as part of their teaching and learning strategy.

Survey metrics lie at the heart of modern Further and Higher Education and although the methodology may change in the future, the central principles of high-quality teaching and learning, value for money and courses which prepare students for both work and for the wider challenges faced will not change. What has become clear in the last few years since the TEF was introduced is that innovation in education is a key aspect for all organisations.

In early 2020, the world was watching the devastation unfolding in China as the new coronavirus (COVID-19) took hold; in the coming months we saw the virus spread to almost every country across the globe. In March 2020, the World Health Organisation declared a pandemic (WHO 2020). Referred to by many as a *black swan* event, the virus was unexpected and hard to predict. The education sector had to change, and quickly. Across universities and colleges, there was a speedy shift to online delivery with digital literacy skills put to the test (Zhou and Wolstencroft 2020). With debates regarding changing admissions policies, academic regulations, exams, assessments and the finances of students and providers, one thing was certain – education was never going back to the way it was before.

1 Towards a new landscape for UK Higher Education

TEF Principles this chapter refers to:

Learning environment: resources and activities to support learning and improve retention, progression and attainment

In 2019, marathon runner Eliud Kipchoge completed the 26.2-mile course in 1 hour, 59 minutes and 40 seconds, a sub-two-hour run which previously had been described as beyond what was humanly possible for athletes (Joyner *et al.* 2011). As has occurred previously when barriers deemed 'impossible' were broken, after a period of incredulity and celebration, the achievement was adopted as the new norm and the impenetrability of the old barrier forgotten about and replaced by a new limitation. As an example of this, 46 days after Roger Bannister broke another 'unbreakable' barrier, the four-minute mile, it was broken again; less than a year later, three athletes in the same race broke four minutes (Taylor 2018) and since then more than a thousand people have followed in Bannister's footsteps with the world record being 17 seconds faster than the four-minute mile barrier.

The idea that the limitations and indeed the norms of our world are a social construct is not a new one (Berger and Luckmann 1966) and is just as applicable to the world of education as to the athletics track. The shared assumptions that make up our view of education are at the heart of how we, as participants, frame the sector and are rooted in both historical events and in the inculcated assumptions of those in and around the sector. Historically, the Further Education sector has been anchored by its founding principles of bringing education to all, technical education to those who need it, and also by its role as a vehicle for social change (Green 1995). This has led to a perception of the sector that embraces a widening participation remit as well as a skills-based imperative which harks back to the principles encouraged by the original Mechanics Institutes set up by George Birkbeck (de Waal and Fremantle 2016). By way of contrast, the first growth of universities from the mid-nineteenth to the early-twentieth century was driven by the twin needs of the world's first post-agrarian society and the first global empire. The move to an industrial economy, based on commerce and a rapid growth in a new prosperous middle class led to a need for more doctors, lawyers and teachers to service the economy. At the same time, the ever-widening Empire required an army of administrators to run the colonies. Both these needs were met by the new civic universities and the development of what Perkins (1990) referred to as a professional society.

External influences within education

Within the Higher Education sector, the disparate nature of UK universities has mitigated against a common culture, but what has been noticeable in the last decade has been a shift in the extent to which outside elements have shaped the culture. Whilst in Further Education, external catalysts for change, such as the regulatory body, the Office for Standards in Education, Children's Services and Skills (Ofsted) and the creation of performance-based league tables, have been an established part of the sector, the Higher Education sector has traditionally been far more resistant to outside influences. The shift away from this independence has come in various forms but most of the influences might be described as being performative in nature (Ball 2003). As an example of this, the Research Excellence Framework (commonly known as the REF) that was first suggested as a replacement for the less prescriptive Research Assessment Exercise in 2007, has come to define how the organisation of research is implemented in UK education. The importance of a good result in the final evaluation is perceived as being paramount to the organisation, as it will help attract greater funds for additional research as well as having a reputational impact on the university. These factors mean that the accepted reality is that a good performance in the REF is what drives decisions on research (Pinar and Unlu 2020). It is not only in the area of research that outside influences frame the environment in which universities operate. The Teaching Excellence Framework (TEF) has created a focus on the quality of teaching, as defined by externally set measures of performance. As with the REF, universities have focused their attention on achieving the best possible outcome, rather than challenging the process, despite concerns as to whether the approach has any positive impact on the student experience (Barkas *et al.* 2017) and its unpopularity with the majority of participants (O'Leary *et al.* 2019).

The argument about the relevance of externally set parameters is an ongoing one but with the REF, TEF and other quality procedures, it is one where educational establishments believe that they have no choice but to comply in order that they are perceived to be achieving a set standard. Given that the success criteria are clearly identified, the likelihood is that there will be a movement towards a more homogenised provision designed to meet these standards and a reluctance to experiment due to the worry that this would not fit into the accepted description of outstanding teaching. Whilst there are arguments to suggest that adopting a standard approach might stop some poor practice from becoming embedded, Simmons (2008) described how this happened in the Further Education sector. In such a diverse sector, trying to create a common approach is fraught with difficulties.

The common approach is particularly challenging when considering the funding mechanisms used in education. Within colleges, funding is a byzantine mixture of rules and incentives but broadly it can be split into three themes: first, 16–18 learners are funded by the Education and Skills Funding Agency (ESFA); secondly, the adult education budget, much aimed at those who need qualifications in English and maths, is administered separately and the priorities reviewed on a regular basis; finally, apprenticeships are also funded by the ESFA and again, this is reviewed on a regular basis. For colleges, which are traditionally funded in a less generous manner than universities, the funding represents their prime motivator in setting up and in the running of courses. As funding is attached to individual students, this creates a market between colleges that has encouraged them to compete. This has had advantages in terms of improving the efficiency of the organisations and getting rid of poor practices (Simmons 2008), and it has also had the effect of promoting an economic imperative over an educational one.

Funding for Higher Education differs across the globe, with notable differences in the UK too. In Scotland, undergraduate students under 25 who are Scottish residents do not have to pay tuition fees. There are fees for those over 25, for students from outside Scotland and for postgraduate study. In Northern Ireland, tuition fees are capped (£4275 in 2020) and full loans are available that are to be repaid from future earnings. University funding in England and Wales has seen near-constant reform over the past few decades. Prior to 1998, when tuition fees were introduced, university fees were state funded with additional support in the form of maintenance grants. When tuition fees were introduced, they were capped at £1000. This tripled to £3000 in 2006 and tripled again to £9000 in 2012; from 2017, the government announced that tuition fees would be linked to inflation (£9250 in 2020). Maintenance grants were removed in 2005 and converted to loans to be repaid from future earned income. Student debt on graduation is higher than ever, adversely affecting students from disadvantaged backgrounds. The incremental move from state-funded to wholly student-funded Higher Education led to the competitive marketisation of the sector. There has been a shift in views of education as a 'citizens' social right' to that of a 'customer exercising choice in paying for a marketable product' (Anderson 2016).

The marketisation and commodification of education

This movement towards a defined product in education is one that has proved controversial. Page (2019) talks about the marketisation and commodification of Higher Education and how a neo-liberalist model has become the dominant driver in decision-making. The latter stresses the importance of competition and the dominance of the economic imperative, whilst commodification has resulted in courses being defined in rigid terms and offered to students with a promise that there will be no variation. When this is combined with the increase in tuition fees and also the move towards viewing students as customers (Guilbault 2016), it is clear that the frames of reference in which the sector operates have changed significantly.

Whilst it could be argued that a standardised offer creates a degree of certainty which reassures students and also helps them make an informed choice prior to starting their studies, the wider issue is that it is likely to limit the perspective of those within the sector. Just as athletes, prior to the groundbreaking runs of both Bannister and Kipchoge, viewed the time barriers subsequently broken as impenetrable, the danger of having very set conditions and structures in education is that it creates artificial boundaries and promotes a culture of conservativism where attempts to redefine processes are discouraged. In many ways, this argument mirrors those in the Lingfield Report into professionalism within Further Education, which argued that it was not a good idea to impose frameworks onto education (in this case, it was the insistence that teachers have a recognised teaching qualification), as it promoted a lack of independent thought and an increased reliance on others (Lingfield 2012).

Case study 1.1: Overcoming barriers in the teaching of mathematics

Judith Darnell, Bedford College

This case study relates to the recognised need to change students' initial perceptions in order to engage learners more effectively. The unit I taught was part of the Educational Practice Foundation Degree and was called 'Developing Mathematics'. It was concerned with supporting and encouraging maths skills in primary-aged children. It had occurred to me that as much as the unit was about supporting my students to develop maths skills in young children, it was first and foremost about fostering a positive view of maths in my students themselves.

It was week one. As I entered the room, I felt the breeze of some heavy sighs. I smiled, panned the room and asked if the students were OK. Silence. Finally one of the students muttered, "Erm ... we're a bit worried because ... well ... because it's MATHS ...'. Fortunately, I had already realised that the thing I needed to do first in order to engage students more effectively and help them to achieve and enjoy the unit was to challenge their own perceptions of mathematics and help them to reflect on and review their own experiences (often negative) before I could move on with any pedagogical approaches, unit assessments or impart practical advice in relation to this controversial subject.

On reflection, I realised that I had subconsciously applied the following framework, which I have named the 'URC' (Unfreeze, Re-lay, Champion). Each point is explained briefly below and followed by an explanation in greater detail underneath.

1 *Unfreeze/dismantle student negative perceptions.* This was achieved by asking students to (a) reflect on their previous experiences of maths, and (b) re-examine the purpose of mathematics within society and specifically for children's everyday lives.

2 *Re-lay foundations and build confidence.* I found that I needed to start to build confidence in students, whilst reaffirming the purpose of the subject (which relates to point 1) and build a positive feeling towards maths through small puzzles, games and examples where students could share their thoughts in a 'safe' place through discussion and practice.

3 *Create champions for the subject.* Students not only needed to feel safe with maths themselves but needed to be taken a step above this where they could be encouraged to use their new-found confidence to build it up in others and to support the development of skills in the pupils they taught.

The 'URC' was mainly underpinned by dialogue which allowed for self-expression, the opportunities to ask questions in small groups as well as offering flexibility in testing different modelling techniques.

As I had foreseen the initial negative reception, the first teaching session was filled with small activities that were specifically designed to help students to reflect on their perceptions. Time was spent discussing students' own childhood memories and students were challenged to pinpoint specific areas of maths that they had found challenging (see point 1). I saw this act of 'unfreezing' negative perceptions as integral to the unit, even though it was not on the threshold criteria or unit outcomes. However, I was confident that although time was short, it was necessary to spend time addressing these previous concerns for students because this allowed the negativity to be dismantled so that students came to think about maths in a new and positive way, which was incredibly valuable for subsequent learning.

This act of 'unfreezing/dismantling' needed to be followed by the laying of a new foundation (see point 2), which was, in effect, a new-found willingness to be open to mathematical ideas and to accept a change in perception of all that they had previously associated with the subject. It also included a reflection on the purpose of maths within society and specifically within other areas of learning to foster a feeling of 'a clean slate' to enable future positive associations to be made to maths. Additionally, students were given small tasks designed to allow them to succeed and to build confidence. Students discussed theories, skills and methods, and were provided with a plethora of examples to ensure maximum opportunity for understanding. This newly-laid foundation, coupled with new-found confidence, could then be built upon and new skills could be successfully gained through repetition, modelling, encouragement and practice. I found that the most effective way to foster confidence was to ask the students to model mathematical problems, to discuss, to rehearse explanations and to expose themselves to the language of mathematics in a dialogic manner whilst keeping the purpose of maths in mind.

Lastly, where the first two points had been met, students were then able to successfully and finally execute point 3, which related to their new-found interest in and passion for passing on their skills to the children with whom they worked. A change to positive thinking allowed the students to be a champion in their support of maths for the pupils they taught. It offered an opportunity to share their skills with confidence. Interestingly, point 3 was the only one that related to the threshold criteria and the learning outcomes for the unit. However, without experiencing the 'unfreezing' and 're-laying' of a new foundation, my feeling is that this 'championing' would have never been achieved, as tempting as it would have been to jump straight into thinking about assessment, especially with the usual time constraints of teaching in Higher Education.

Students appeared to have appreciated the opportunities that this framework provided. Student J reported:

"My whole perception of maths changed through this unit. Reflection was really beneficial at the start and I loved the fact that the lessons were so practical. We were challenged by puzzles, were able to discuss them and were then encouraged to come up with our own, and this helped me to understand the process and importance of them. Being able to think of different strategies really tested us and made it more fun! I could then go and use these puzzles at school. Being able to challenge the children and seeing them attempting the problems was satisfying. I think I now have a better understanding of these problems and have enjoyed doing them myself, which has supported my pedagogy and I now enjoy problem-solving myself as well as teaching maths to others."

The changing role of the student

Judith's experience is a classic example of changing students' frames of reference. Our reality is shaped by our previous experiences and as can be seen in the above case study, this shapes our view of what we are met with. The changing role of the student is also a factor when we look at the frames of reference adopted in the sector. Tomlinson (2017) notes that students view themselves as consumers of education and this has had a significant impact on their perception of their experiences. With the advent of both increased tuition fees and the focus on performance measures, this has caused a shift in power between students and organisations, with the former now looking for increased 'value for money' (OfS 2019c). This shift in power between students and universities is clear when the strategy for the OfS is studied. An extract from their policy document reads: 'Our primary measure of value for money will be based on the perceptions of students and graduates. This will allow us to monitor progress without imposing our own definition of value for money on students' (OfS 2019c). The inference of this is that it is up to students to define what they view as 'value for money'. This has several potential pitfalls, not least that students do not always have the experience to be able to judge this aspect, as they lack a comparative frame of reference.

The trend towards a more homogeneous product for education, the increased use of quantitative measures, the introduction of a host of quality measures, the rise in the tuition fee and Tomlinson's (2017) assertion that students are consumers, has created a landscape that has altered the balance of power between students and the organisation. Whereas education used to be something that students had little influence over, the onus is now on universities to ensure that students are satisfied with the provision. This shift has led to a number of changes in approach from UK institutions that have fundamentally altered the relationship between students and education. Two of the key ones are examined below.

Two changes in education

The first change revolves around the desire to define what students' educational experience will consist of and to ensure that there is a homogenised product that can be sold to potential students. Within Higher Education, this can manifest itself in various ways, including via the publicly available information about courses and the availability of a charter of rights for students. This changes the relationship, as students are given clear guidance as to what will happen on their course and they are encouraged to comment on this at regular stages throughout their course via module evaluations, course questionnaires and nationally set surveys. Organisations then respond to concerns or any variations in the programme delivered. This places power with the students and, returning to the OfS policy, the expectation is that students will judge the programme based on their initial expectations. Whilst this can be seen as a limiting factor when reviewing education, with any changes needing to be communicated to students in advance and the onus being on the institution to respond to students, it also creates an opportunity for establishments to improve communication with their students and help guide them towards understanding what constitutes value for money. Returning to a previous theme, whilst the OfS's desire to have students define what is meant by value for money might be viewed as a valid attempt to introduce marketisation into the sector, the fact that students are generally not able to compare their experiences with anything else is a problem and one that might well be rectified by the organisation working alongside students to explain and guide them.

The second change is in the way organisations approach the marketing of their offer. Given the neo-liberal market they work within, the concept of competition is deeply engrained, and the techniques used are often more closely associated with the marketing that takes place within the private sector rather than an approach that espouses the benefits of education. Given that one of the stated purposes of the Further and Higher Education Act 1992 was to ensure that best practice from the private sector was transferred to the publicly funded parts of the education sector (DfE 1992), this is not surprising. However, this has led to a number of problems. First, there is much debate about whether the practice identified in the private sector is better than existing practice or indeed relevant to the sector (Thompson and Wolstencroft 2018). Secondly, it also means that when marketing courses, organisations tend to treat them in a similar way they would a product. Now whilst there has been a movement towards homogeneity, it is still the case that students' experiences on a course will vary according to a multitude of factors (indeed, it could be argued that this is a positive, as it increases the personalisation of the experience) but any variation is likely to conflict with a marketing approach that stresses a 'product' as that which requires tangible, measurable outputs, something that is difficult to achieve.

Different organisations have approached this in different ways and there has been a marked divide between the Further and Higher Education sectors, as well as within the Higher Education sector itself. Our second case study looks at how this issue is addressed in a traditional, 'red brick' university.

Case study 1.2: Managing student expectations at a 'red brick' university

John Gough, Centre for Lifelong Learning (CLL), University of Warwick

In common with the rest of the sector, we find that the influence of pre-tertiary education (and wider life experience) on students' expectations of their student experience is considerable. For more 'traditional students', the performativity that schools and colleges face means that the grade profile of learners is important and that affects the students. Changes in the National Curriculum and the 'academisation' of education provision means that academic work has become very formulaic, for example in terms of the format and language required when completing exams. It means that students, when they come to us, can expect quite a bit of guidance on how the work should look and they are often focused on the marking scheme, often for reassurance. Their aim is always to get a 'good degree'; in addition, many of their attitudes are driven by the changes in student finances with debt being a key issue. Learners in the CLL are more 'non-traditional', with 64% of our students being over the age of 25; and their education and life experience brings with it a richness and diversity that also shapes their hopes, expectations and anxieties.

We find that students can have high expectations about the level of tutor support for drafting essays and answers. I receive a lot of drafts sent through by email. This can be due to understandable stress and anxiety, often in relation to producing the 'right' answer or format. I try to be helpful, whilst emphasising that as a policy we do not pre-mark. There is a further dynamic. Some students are very adept at being able to navigate their way through online resources but what has surprised me is the number of emails where students have asked to send stuff that is freely available. Students seem to expect more things, so if a link is broken on our virtual learning environment, for example, they often expect the tutor to fix it very quickly, instead of using their initiative to find the resource. We tend to spend a lot of time orientating our students to their learning environment (including the digital environment), so increasingly the innovation is about understanding where students are at rather than where we expect them to be, especially in terms of competence with technology.

The Early Childhood Studies course we run has a lot of individuals who are working part time and so the innovation there is to deliver the course on a blended basis with face-to-face teaching being in the evening so there is a lot of study support for these students. The extent of our learning technology and student support can be key in helping students to succeed.

Within the CLL, we see students who have wide-ranging needs, and so we work hard to support these. For the university as a whole, students are *selected* rather than just recruited, and so we can expect a greater degree of self-sufficiency. This does vary of course but was different to my previous (post-92) university experience, where students arrive with a wide variety of qualifications that don't necessarily prepare them for a traditional assessment diet. There is also a strong linkage of theory to practice in post-92, particularly in areas such as health and social care; and many courses have work experience or more formal placements as standard. The latter is less prevalent here where a more traditional student experience is in place, though this is changing.

In summary, we see students as partners in the creation of an educational experience. They are customers when they are paying for halls of residence or when they are buying things, but they are not simply buying a degree. This is where our initial induction and orientation provision is so key in agreeing the overall learning contract. They are a partner not just a customer, though when under stress they might sound like one! This is understandable, but it can be disappointing when they are too often (and only) described as such. They are partners.

If we accept that Tomlinson's (2017) assertion of students as consumers is correct, then a subtle shift of emphasis is needed. Whilst a customer is generally assumed to be purchasing an item of set specifications, using the word consumer implies that the student will be a participant in the process. They are not merely conducting a transaction; they are part of a longer relationship. This suggests that a service marketing approach would be more beneficial, as would an approach that encourages partnership between the organisation and its students.

A final limitation that exists within the current Further and Higher Education sector relates to the teaching methods used. Many alternative techniques are discussed within this book but at the heart of the debate is the argument about how we should frame learning. Whilst much of the UK education system is based upon pedagogical principles, which put the lecturer at the heart of the learning process, post-16 education has tended to be organised with andragogical principles in mind (Knowles 1984), which hold that the answers come from within students and the job of the lecturer is merely to facilitate the process of learning. Whilst this approach has been the dominant ideology within Higher Education in particular, it does require a certain set of skills from students experiencing it for the first time. Given the exam factory approach of much of compulsory education in the UK, this can prove to be problematic (Coffield and Williamson 2011).

As with many of the issues discussed in this chapter, students' expectations are framed by both their previous experiences and their environment, so the imperative when looking at teaching and learning is to ensure that students are prepared for their experiences. Expecting students who have been used to a culture that stressed exam results and passivity in sessions to engage in their learning and take control of the experience is unrealistic and is likely to lead to confusion and resentment – hence, the transition period at the start of their studies is a key part of students' studies. It is also not just the concerns of the students that need to be addressed. Within a performative culture, there is often a fear amongst educators that trying something innovative is a risk and that if it does not go well, the evaluation results will decline, and this can impact on the lecturer. Hence, it is important for the organisation to address this and find ways of encouraging innovation, taking away the worry, whilst ensuring that the quality of provision is upheld.

Returning one last time to the field of athletics. The construct of the norms and the limitations for the marathon have recently been reset as a result of Kipchoge's remarkable run. This has meant that his competitors' expectations have changed as they readjust to the new external influences on their race. In many ways, this approach is similar in education and it is up to organisations to take control of this process and ensure that students are guided through it. Any externally imposed requirements, whilst important, need to be balanced by a wider understanding that allows students to accept the environment they are in, understand it and also ensure that they are not limited unnecessarily.

Key takeaways

Whilst it is easy to argue that change in education is hardly a new concept, what is new is the increase in external influences and their success in shaping the current landscape within which colleges and universities operate. This can be seen as a threat with the increased use of data, the external quality measures and the renewed focus on 'value for money'. However, it might also be seen as an opportunity for organisations to help define the environment. Many of the concepts that shape the student experience are nebulous in nature and with students having limited experience on which to draw, organisations can work with students to help them understand the process and also to help them come to realistic judgements.

There are three main areas where organisations can take action to help shape the landscape:

1 Work with students to help define education and to move away from an unrealistic expectation of homogeneity of experience.

2 Ensure that communications with students stress the fact that the relationship should be more akin to a service marketing approach rather than the marketing of a product.

3 Encourage innovation in teaching and learning and remove the fear for lecturers in trying something new, whilst also preparing students for alternative ways of learning.

Inspired by this chapter? Why not try ...

- *adopting andragogical teaching approaches*
- *adapting the induction of students to take into account their previous experiences*
- *adopting a communication strategy to students that is both two-way and coherent in approach*
- *challenging staff to showcase innovative teaching approaches*
- *exploring a Universal Design for Learning (UDL)*

Part 1

Teaching Quality

2 Learning lessons in observation from student teachers

*By Georgina Gretton, Liverpool John Moores University –
with thanks to Liverpool John Moores University final-
year primary student teachers for their reflections*

TEF Principles this chapter refers to:

Teaching quality: teaching that stimulates and challenges students, and maximises engagement with their studies

Evidencing learning is the main business of working in education (Freebody 2003), with the aim of any professional programme being to ensure that students feel equipped with the skills they need to be outstanding professionals. To achieve this, many institutions mandate that their staff are observed in their professional practice and that they observe others to ensure that they are exposed to a range of teaching techniques and that they are supported to reflect on their own teaching.

This chapter aims to explore the ways in which observations are used and could be used to improve professional practice for institutions, Higher Education professionals and students alike. This will be achieved by exploring the experiences of a group of student teachers for whom observation is both central not only to their development, but also to the assessment of their practice. Students training to be teachers observe the practice of more experienced professionals, who will be known in this chapter as 'more knowledgeable others' (MKOs) – a term used by Vygotsky (1978) – in order to gain quality improvement. Straight away, this is an interesting juxtaposition with the more common role of observation that falls under the guise of quality assurance. The specific foci of inexperienced observers and the role of observation in securing quality improvement both appear to be areas that are yet to be explored in depth. It is hoped that this chapter will provide a degree of generalisability or at least a starting point for improving the existing observation processes for areas of Higher Education that have already adopted the tool, such as medicine, coaching and engineering, but also a source of information for those who are considering it as a learning tool.

The case for observation

The effectiveness of observation as a learning technique is proven (Fish 1995; Schön 2009; O'Leary 2013). It allows people to study processes and practices in natural settings, prompting them to collect evidence as to what goes on in these settings, which they can use to conceptualise what effective practice may look like. The premise of observation in securing learning for the observer appears to be that illustrative examples of theory are provided through exposure to the professional practice of others, and that in turn, students will then master and demonstrate it themselves. Scaffolding such as guidance and modelling from the MKO should eventually retreat as the 'novice' acquires the necessary skills to work independently.

Didau (2018) suggests that the observer will always learn more than the observee. Consequently, observation can be viewed as developmental in that the observer is offered opportunities to increase their awareness and evaluation of professional practices through interaction with MKOs, which in turn should stimulate and verify elements of the observer's own practice. When discussing professional learning, Hascher *et al.* (2004) claim that field experiences are the best way to acquire professional knowledge and competence, while Tenenberg (2014) states that learning in and through practice is an important way for development to occur.

Defining observation

Observation can take on varied forms: from engagement in a complete demonstration through to a focused component or a snippet of time. It is suggested that observations should be pre-planned and the foci discussed to allow opportunities to identify and collect specific evidence from observation events. Several elements appear to be consistent across observation procedures, in that they must have: a purpose; a definition of professional and learning behaviours; a focus; training; a setting; an allocated time; and a method of recording appropriate to the processing and analysis of any collected evidence (Anderson and Burns 1989). Wragg (2011) summarises that effective observation should suit the purpose, timing and context of the situation; however, the complexity of these variables would suggest that no single process may actually exist.

User beware!

Although widely adopted across many professional sectors, there are concerns regarding the effectiveness of observation for securing quality improvement through field experience. O'Leary (2012) suggests that there is no universal truth or normalisation of practice as to what people are expected to see and gain from the tool of observation. Concerns such as those of O'Leary were validated when working with my own students conducting observations of their MKOs. These concerns tended to fall into two groups regarding whether the trainees were equipped with the appropriate skills to use the tool and, if they were equipped to do so, whether the learning was robust enough to have any impact. There appeared to be a high degree of variability in its success and deployment across students who, although part of the same programme cohort, were then distributed across many different settings. As any professional is sure to do, research was consulted to help unravel these conundrums and inform effective ways forward; however, much of the research was irrelevant, focusing on quality assurance aspects with more experienced observers. As such, questions were asked directly of the students in order to better understand their needs and improve the processes and support that could be offered to them.

Consequently, final-stage undergraduates were chosen to participate in a project aimed at gaining insight into the purposes and processes of observation by asking them to reflect on whether they felt equipped professionally for what the process requires them to see and understand. These students were deemed appropriate for the project because they had the most placement experience to be able to reflect both professionally and with accuracy upon their experiences as they neared the end of their training, having largely already developed their craftsperson competency (Moore 2004) in earlier phases of training.

Observations about observation

Observation appears to be complex and highly subjective, which may be attributed to trying to capture the dynamic nature of social processes, seeing many things that happen simultaneously (Freeman 1982, cited in Swan 1993). Hiebert *et al.* (2007) offer that competence in the relevant subject matter knowledge of the observed event, should equate to better competence with observation, as there is an increased capacity to identify practice, analyse practice and, consequently, improve practice. Freeman (1982, cited in Swan 1993) would perhaps question whether less advanced observers will be able to identify these components in a competent enough manner to secure learning, with Didau (2018) suggesting that it may only be possible to see a mechanical application of methods, which are a reflection of an MKO's interpretation of a process or concept. Compounding this issue, Richards and Farrell (2011) outline how observation is based on the assumptions that competent performance is evident, that an observee's thoughts can be inferred from their actions, and that the observer understands the situation that the observation is conducted within (Caughlan and Heng 2014): assumptions which should all perhaps be treated with caution, particularly with new and emerging professionals.

Not only is there a need for content knowledge and training in observation, but there also appears to be a need for a basic level of competency of professional skills. Fish (1995) and Sellars (2017) offer the professional skill of reflection as one means of investigating and theorising practice. They define it as a systematic and critical process involving creative thinking with the intention of understanding in order to improve or change future actions. Observation without reflection makes it difficult to enact changes to secure quality improvement. Subsequent responses to reflection are known as the process of reflexivity (Sellars 2017). Therefore, alongside a basic understanding of the subject matter, Behets (1993) suggests that observers need appropriate training in professional skills to be able to record data objectively and form analysis constructively in order to then be able to action the findings into practice. Unfortunately, training in the field of observation can be considered arbitrary at best (Peake 2006).

Next, let us move on to the impact of observation and how imitation does not always indicate secure learning. Some of the student teachers that I work with appear to struggle to move beyond what Paulien *et al.* (2002) deem to be an imitation or cloning of their mentors without mastering the skills and understanding required to enact them independently. For some students, although performance of required actions was evident, the rationale and explanation were lacking, while for other students, they were yet to even be able to replicate the observed practice for themselves. Without a repertoire of knowledge and understanding and the professional skills to reflect and analyse practice, experience appears to remain as ritual knowledge of experiences and procedures and fails to develop into principled knowledge rooted in understanding. However, Richardson (2004, cited in Podmore 2012) argues that imitation of behaviours stemming from observation will eventually move to other naturally occurring situations, indicating a transfer of learning (Hendry and Oliver 2012), which Swan (1993) sees as a lag between what there is an awareness or understanding of and what can be implemented at that time. Zulaikha *et al.* (2017) suggest that any mastery of practical professional skills is only achieved a few years after the learning journey has begun, which raises questions about how effective the use of observation could possibly ever be in earlier experiences.

Swan's (1993) idea of a time lag between performance and understanding is important, as it could be assumed that understanding actually occurs at the point of performance. Feiman-Nemser (1998) suggests that expertise develops through a learning curve and is not achieved during training or early experiences. This claim was substantiated by Oser and Oelkers (2001) in their study of teacher training, in which professional skills and standards were not acquired by students on practice. Pavlov (1927) would have questioned whether learning acquisition can ever be externally checked, as he deemed it to be introspective and subjective, with only the learner really being able to observe the internal process of learning; however, he also defined learning as a change in behaviour, which can be observed through behavioural 'performances'. Jenkins (2014) suggests that these performances must be re-enacted to demonstrate learning and subsequent transfer of learning have occurred. Hiebert *et al.* (2002) add that the insularity of isolated experiences must be overcome so that professional learning may be accumulated, connections made and transferred across contexts.

To develop understanding to inform professional performance, isolated experiences within observation are judged by Pressick-Kilborn and te Riele (2008) and Gould (2012) to have limited impact, as learning occurs through critical reflection on evidence obtained from a variety of sources, not just in one observation experience. However, Hiebert and his colleagues (2002) suggest that single observational experiences are small enough units of complexity to allow analysis of the interconnected components of practice and the subsequent intended professional learning to be manageable. Even if they were not, Thomson *et al.* (2015) argue that learning from 'just watching' can be effective, as it allows focus on content and context, which in turns prompts the process of an individual's attempt to make meaning and find their own interpretation. The students from the study have access to predetermined institutional observation schedules but are largely undirected in how or when to deploy these frameworks when collecting or analysing evidence from their experiences. This lack of direction may further contribute to missed learning, as Oosterheert and Vermunt (2001) state that most observers are not directed to construct any professional knowledge that sits outside their existing frame of reference, meaning that observation is a tool for consolidation of learning rather than extension of learning (Haggar *et al.* 1993). Indeed, many professionals who are already acting as observers, use schedules and carry out accompanying reflections that are often within repeated contexts linking to their area of professional 'expertise'.

Learning lessons in observation from the student teachers

Students told me that:

> *Professional knowledge and skills are gained on a trajectory that observation must acknowledge and develop alongside.*

In the students' own words:

> *"My learning is facilitated through observation because of a greater understanding of what I am doing and why I am doing it"*

> *"You didn't really know what to do in an observation during earlier stages because you don't even really know what you are looking at!"*

> *"Now, I can access the whole story, rather than the pieces"*

The students reflected that in the earlier stages of their course when using observation, the processes relied on low inference factors that have greater transparency (O'Leary 2013) and were able to capture practice through categorising variables in heavily structured schedules (Croll 1986). O'Leary (2013) states that factors that are high inference offer greater subjectivity but less transparency and are generally harder to capture. To this end, the institution offers students guided proformas in earlier phases. Although arguably reductionist in nature, they enable the observers to be able to translate a complex social process and its associated events into simple figures and categories for judgement (Ball 2003) that may be beneficial in isolating components of complex practice (Hiebert *et al.* 2002) for understanding.

Having secured a greater knowledge base to reflect with, the students deemed these schedules to be 'superficial' and 'passive' but acknowledged that they are suitable as a somewhat temporary scaffold in supporting the capture of the knowledge and skills that some observers are yet to possess. They reflected on this with frustration, as this model of conducting and capturing observation could be argued to reduce complex dynamics into a linear and rateable system, even though students were keen to access the greater depth that they knew existed (O'Leary 2013). Aspects such as complex decision-making, professional judgement and practical wisdom are not able to be broken down into absolute, rateable routines and there is a need for further processes to complement and support observation (Fish 1995). These further processes only seemed to emerge in later stages of their observational journey, when they had an independent level of knowledge and skill to develop them.

The students outlined processes that they had developed which were seemingly individual and self-directed, enabling them to collect evidence to analyse and secure their professional understanding (Bell *et al.* 1985). Limited numbers of students reported that they do not collect or record any evidence during the process, rendering observation as informal and self-directed, whilst others stated that they always record observational activities. When exploring students' use of observation schedules, Jenkins' (2014) findings are representative of the comments of the students, in that notes taken during observations decrease as practice experience alongside professional knowledge and understanding increase. Any schedules that were still used perhaps may have connected to an element of 'strategic compliance', in that observational processes were still rooted in more guided and formal expectations from earlier in their course. This concept is perhaps also valid when considering the role of observation in quality assurance practices and is often relevant to professionals working with observation who are often directed to use feedback and evidence processes using a guided observation schedule that is subsequently shared with other relevant parties.

Foucault (1980) suggests that there is no one correct way to observe and that people will simply develop their own process that will work for them, as learning is subjective, constructed individually and cognitive in nature. Croll (1986) remarks that for an observation to be effective and purposeful for the observer, the focus of the observation must relate to their existing abilities and knowledge and that any purposeful, meaningful learning beyond basic competence will take place after qualification (Mena *et al.* 2017), or towards the end of a training programme when observers develop the ability to reflect (McIntyre and Hagger 1993). Arguably, this renders any gains in professional learning through observation whilst training as superficial, and largely limited to imitation (Hascher *et al.* 2004). This perhaps is due to the fact that such professional knowledge and understanding could be defined as a 'complex web of variables' (Davis and Fantozzi 2016), with Strevens (1974) adding that consequently, observation is also highly complex and requires knowledge rooted in the understanding of practice and a repertoire of experience. Even when completed by 'more knowledgeable others' (Vygotsky 1978), it incurs an equally high demand due to its difficult nature (Nutbrown 2011). In tasking students to observe the practice of more knowledgeable others (Vygotskty 1978) from the offset, there is perhaps an implied and misplaced assumption that these elements are already in place, allowing them to be able to identify elements of practice in the first instance, and then be able to understand them and use them to inform their own professional improvement (Caughlan and Heng 2014). This seems to correlate with students' comments around trajectory progression, not only in their knowledge and understanding but also their skill set.

Students told me that:

> In-field observations consolidate and extend pre-existing knowledge.

In the students' own words:

> "You can learn everything in university, but until you see it in practice, you have no idea"
>
> "You see theory in practice, reflect on it and consider how you can implement it"
>
> "When you see it, you'll learn how to practically translate all that theory"

Hiebert et al. (2002) define theory as an abstract notion, free of context. There is a need for observers to understand not only practical knowledge but also the complexities of theoretical knowledge behind the practices (Hudson et al. 2013).

Students often struggle to make the connections between theory and practice, and they speak extensively about the need for illustrations of theoretical constructs to aid understanding (Zeichner 2010; Sjølie 2014). Students appear to use observation to illustrate and consolidate what they already know, stating that until the point of seeing theory in practice-based experience, the constructs cannot be understood. O'Leary (2012) concurs with this, saying that there is an expectation that when students see illustrative examples of theory through practice, they will then master and demonstrate it themselves. And Leinhardt et al. (1995) argue that the two elements – theory and practice – are as important as one another and must go hand in hand. These comments connect to Gestalt theory, in that learning must encompass the whole picture to reveal the relationships between the parts.

Students only appeared to value theoretical constructs when they were deemed to be authentic. Within a context-rich environment, Hiebert et al. (2002) and Jenkins (2014) feel that it is this specificity of the situation and context that actually allows theoretical understanding to emerge through observations in the field. The majority of the students from the project agreed with these findings and stated that observation supports their development of campus-based constructs, which appears to help students navigate the complexity of professional dynamics (Britzman 2003). However, Jenkins (2014) states that students can only benefit from observational experiences to develop elements of practice, should a basic grasp of the subject matter already be present. This links to the previous finding regarding the trajectory of securing professional knowledge and understanding.

Caution is advised regarding this trajectory, as Coe (2014) suggests that untrained observers, yet to secure their professional knowledge, will often struggle to accurately judge the effectiveness of an experience, and can often misinterpret practice, which is a subjective perception (Wragg 2011). This may not only be due to the trajectory of the student, but also the suggestion that learning is invisible and can only be inferred from observed events (Caughlan and Heng 2014; Coe 2014). If a student can replicate the same performance, this does not necessarily demonstrate that they have learned anything – as performance is measurable but learning can only be inferred (Didau 2018). Hiebert *et al.* (2007) suggest it may be better for reflection to sit outside of the observation experience due to the demands it places on the observer, perhaps back in campus-based sessions where accuracy can be monitored and further development and training in observation skills can occur.

Observation facilitates the construction of learner identity as a professional through discourse, and occasional discontent.

In the students' own words:

"It is independent when you start moving towards the kind of professional you want to be"

"It shapes the way you conduct yourself"

"You need to understand it, to develop and to fit into the mould"

"You just take what you want from it and there are some things that you think are great but it's not going to work for me"

"You can implement appropriate aspects so that you are then treated as a professional"

Students mentioned their own identity developing through observation and acknowledged that this is not a static entity but has changed over time, using terms such as 'becoming', 'now' and offering direct comparisons to earlier phases of their observational journeys. Sachs (2005) and Coldron and Smith (1999) support the notion that identity is not a static entity but is created in a formative manner through a variety of experiences. Identity cannot be taught or imposed but is negotiated through a variety of experiences and the associated meanings that they are assigned (Sachs 2005). Coldron and Smith (1999) suggest that a wide range of observational situations could be presented to the observer to enable them to interact, build meaning and develop their identity.

Professional dialogue and reasoning appear powerful in supporting the formation of learner identity (Alsup 2006), through a variety of external experiences and links to narratives of practice. Interestingly, long-term professional development is also most successful when based around collaboration linking to shared foci for learning, in which observation is also well placed (Hiebert *et al.* 2002). LaBoskey (2004) suggests that professional knowledge is best understood and transformed in collaboration with other professionals, with the discussion and information rendering the scene of the observation as intelligible (Tenenberg 2014).

Professional discourse arising from observation supports the development of practice, as it provides access to 'habits of the mind' (Dewey 1933), making the tacit, explicit; bringing not just the what but the how and why to the surface (Hudson *et al.* 2013). However, interactions surrounding observation will be locally set, with Hiebert *et al.* (2002) expressing caution, as the information being used to facilitate learning is context-sensitive and often richly descriptive. They elaborate that there is also no evidence that the knowledge being generated in these localised experiences is correct or useful, or that the MKO can link these experiences back to the observer's existing frame of reference (Hiebert *et al.* 2002). As such, it would be advisable for institutions to have mechanisms in place to monitor the accuracy of learning arising from such experiences.

The role of the institution in observation was relevant again, with student comments linking exclusively to observation conducted through field experiences and did not acknowledge discussion and reasoning connected to observation within campus-based sessions through video footage or demonstrations. A recurring theme was that field experiences were held in higher esteem than campus-based sessions, as for their professional identity to be legitimately sanctioned, observers must prove competence in the field (Smith 2005). Lacey (1977, cited in Smith 2005) discusses how less experienced observers are particularly susceptible to the influence of the community of practice, feeling a need for positive regard, leading to conformity and cooperation rather than confronting aspects that do not suit their emerging identities, in what Lacey coins 'strategic compliance', whereby possible tensions are reduced and self-efficacy is increased. This may limit opportunities for in-field observation to have the potential to challenge existing personal and professional beliefs and form identity through tensions presented in observational contexts that do not sit comfortably with current professional knowledge resulting in a revised viewpoint. This draws parallels with the work of Piaget (1952) when considering how learning has to accommodate and assimilate in response to periods of disequilibrium.

Key takeaways

Themes emerging from student experiences appeared to suggest that observation must follow a trajectory in line with the observers' professional skills and understanding; that the process and purpose is highly contextualised to the knowledge base of individuals; and appears connected to discourse arising through reflection and analysis of evidence that helps form learner identities.

Is the observer equipped to conduct observation for securing quality improvement?

Students reflected on how their professional skills and knowledge had evolved over their training and how it correlated to their work with observation. In earlier phases, students stated that their professional knowledge was a barrier to the process and rendered it as superficial and passive through the use of guided observation schedules, which have evolved to become self-directed and unguided in nature. As professional understanding built, students' awareness of the complexities of processes and knowledge did too. However, this did not always result in their ability to identify aspects of practice or implement them, but it did serve to consolidate what they already knew and offered illustrative examples of practice, further supported through discussion with the observed.

What is the impact of observation in securing quality improvement?

In-field observational opportunities could be considered as an experience through which observers are able to bring together the disconnected domains (Sjølie 2014) of practice and theoretical constructs (Hiebert *et al.* 2002), rooting them in a rich context allowing for the transference of learning to their own practice (Tenenberg 2014). Positive and negative observational experiences were of value in providing the opportunity for discussion of discontent and tensions, serving to further consolidate or prompt reflection and reflexivity on the part of the observers, in turn linking to the construction of learner identity.

Inspired by this chapter? Why not try ...

- *developing observation schedules with the observers who will use them*
- *incorporating observational experiences within campus-based sessions to explore how discourse can further understanding and identity construction*
- *directing observational experiences to secure and complement existing competencies*
- *directing observational experiences outside the current frame of reference to extend existing competencies*
- *developing a mechanism for verifying the accuracy of field-based analysis and interpretation of observational evidence*

3 Developing new learning resources

TEF Principles this chapter refers to:

Teaching quality: teaching that stimulates and challenges students, and maximises engagement with their studies

The alarm goes, you reach over to switch if off, swing your legs off the bed, left then right, brush your teeth, shower, put your socks on left, then right … a typical morning routine, a variation of which is carried out all over the world. The routine allows a person to ease themselves into the stresses of the day without having to put too much thought into the process and it provides structure to the dawning of a new day, at a time when many people are not looking to exert themselves too much. Our routines are embedded in our psyche and often follow classic behaviourist theory, which means that the pattern is well established and, crucially, does not require too much in the way of thought (Lazaric 2011).

In many ways, there is nothing wrong with having a morning routine – if we had to think about every moment of time between waking up and leaving for work, not only would it extend the time it takes to complete the chores that need to be done, it would also rely on us thinking things through rather more than we in fact do. When we get to work, however, simple repetitions of behaviourist patterns become more difficult to justify. Of course, there are some jobs that can thrive with this approach; repetitive tasks, for example, such as those completed on a production line, require manual dexterity or the ability to respond to a stimulus at a given speed – anything that lends itself perfectly to a behaviourist approach. Within education, however, repetition is not really to be encouraged or valued. The capricious nature of education policy, the importance of ensuring that teaching is informed by the latest research, as well as the desire to keep pushing the boundaries of new knowledge that is part of the *raison d'être* of universities mean that repetitious behaviour is neither desirable nor encouraged.

Despite this, there is a tendency to view the UK Higher Education sector as conservative in nature (Dearlove 1995). Michael Gove, newly appointed as

Secretary of State for Education, memorably described the education sector as 'the Blob' after the Steve McQueen film that featured an amoeba that was engulfing the world. He was referring to the intransigence that permeated much of the compulsory sector, a situation that was fuelled by bureaucracy and a distrust of outsiders, but the reality is that this description could also be applied to the post-compulsory sector. Universities and colleges have histories that go back many centuries, and although many organisations talk about their agility and responsiveness to external stakeholders, inside the story is rather different. The paradigm adopted tends to be linked to continuity and maintenance of standards, despite the suggestions made to the outside world.

Within education, much of the research conducted has its roots in social science and this provides the context in which to understand the paradigm adopted in the sector. The notion of paradigm, in its modern usage, can be traced back to Kuhn (1962), who took the word from the Greek *paradeigma*. The English translation of this is 'example' or 'exemplar' (Göktürk 2005), although it is now more commonly used as a conceptualisation or set of beliefs of how we understand the world (Kuhn 1962; Atkinson 2013). The conceptualisation that is used within Further and Higher Education is that it does not always welcome change and with the emphasis on tradition, typified by such events as graduation, which relies on archaic robes and rituals, changing the paradigm can prove to be a difficult task.

Changing paradigms

In his RSA lecture 'Changing Education Paradigms', Ken Robinson talked about the way in which educational establishments were meeting the challenges of the future by doing exactly what they have done in the past (Robinson 2010). Robinson's speech, which covered areas as diverse as teaching methods, assessment and the increasing prevalence of students with special educational needs, highlighted the landscape in which education operates and challenged it to change to meet the needs of the students and to alter the paradigm in which it operates. The frustration that Robinson articulates about inertia within education can be mirrored, on a smaller scale, within each educational establishment. Although there are some superb examples of innovative, inclusive practice (many of which are discussed within this book), there are also plentiful examples where despite encouragement, courses, modules and lessons have not changed. There are many reasons for this, some of which are genuine, some linked to a perception that change is difficult to enact in post-compulsory education, and some that are a combination of the two.

An example of perceived intransigence revolves around university quality assurance structures. These generally require courses to be reviewed on a regular basis to ensure that they remain current, research informed and relevant to students. These procedures often culminate in an event which reviews the updated course and focuses on the ways in which it will meet the needs of students. Whilst these events provide many staff with the opportunity to embrace alternative approaches, some talk about institutional barriers that prevent them implementing their ideas, or byzantine rules that need to be navigated before change can be embedded, whilst others remain unaware of the opportunities to change. Returning to our thoughts on an established routine, if you have done the same thing multiple times in the past, it is difficult to then change your approach. The idea of education as transformative is an established one (Mezirow 1997) but that tends to refer to students rather than any transformative practice amongst lecturers.

Barriers to changing the paradigm

As well as the perception that quality assurance procedures are difficult to navigate when trying to introduce more innovative methods of teaching and learning, universities and colleges must also be aware of a number of other barriers to overcome when looking at changing the paradigm and developing a new approach within the organisation.

The first barrier relates to institutional factors. When designing a new course, it is generally accepted that for each module, a specification will need to be written which covers the agreed content. This has become especially important with the introduction of the Office for Students (OfS) and the increased view of students as consumers (Bunce *et al.* 2017; Tomlinson 2017), and means that the focus is on what is 'deliverable'. Whilst innovation is often encouraged in the guidance documentation, the formality of these events and the fact that in many organisations there is a list of assessments that are deemed acceptable means that, for many lecturers, the barriers that need to be broken down before introducing innovative resources are often ones they are unwilling to overcome. These institutional barriers are reinforced by the views of students. Returning to Robinson's (2010) talk, he shows how students have become used to a curriculum that often lacks creativity and this means that any attempt to introduce change is met by suspicion. The measurement of a module's success often has an impact on the lecturer and when looking at this combination of factors, it should be no surprise that many lecturers decide to 'play it safe'.

The second barrier identified is a lack of knowledge and this barrier is one that many academics struggle to overcome. Whilst engagement with the latest research via conferences or continuous professional development is commonplace, most of these activities focus upon subject knowledge rather than pedagogical approaches that are viewed as innovative.

So, what can we do about this? How do we change routines and alter the paradigm? The first thing to address is any conservative culture within the organisation and to encourage innovation and alternative approaches. Given that organisations are governed by metrics that are viewed as vital for the successful future of the organisation, many pass on the importance of these quantitative measures to their staff in the form of targets and ways of measuring success. This in turn means that this is what staff focus upon. Whilst in the current climat it is not possible to move away from these targets, by focusing attention on the end goal, rather than the process, the message that is conveyed to staff is that this is what matters rather than the process. Changing this perception, making lecturers aware that if the teaching they do is of a high quality then the metrics will fall into place, is a challenging task but as we can see from our first case study, it is one that has many benefits when lecturers can see how changing their approach can change the dynamics of what they do.

Case study 3.1: Encouraging new approaches

Martin Jenkins, Head of Academic Development, Coventry University

Teaching excellence and enhancing the student learning experience are now clear expectations within the Higher Education sector and can be evidenced through the institutional strategies adopted within the sector. These expectations are drivers for innovation in practice, often through the use of technology, within the sector. However, it is also apparent that while there is innovation, it is only having only a minimal impact on overall teaching and learning practices within the Higher Education sector. The UCISA Teaching Enhanced Learning surveys show how the use of technology has had limited impact in changing practices (Walker *et al*. 2017). Selwyn (2014) discusses how innovation happens in the liminal spaces at the margins and does not impact the mainstream.

So, what strategies can be employed to engage academic staff with new approaches to teaching and learning? Unsurprisingly, this requires a range of approaches and they need to recognise the different context of individuals, disciplines and institutions. This will mean challenging an individual's values and beliefs of teaching and learning, and providing a supportive environment but also clear drivers and incentives. The Academic Development team uses a variety of approaches to develop staff and encourage innovation and enhancement of the student learning experience. This could be seen as being provided through different levels.

Underpinning our support is the desire to seek to develop our staff as scholarly practitioners and to understand how their own values and beliefs inform their approaches to teaching and learning. Teaching and the support of learning in UK Higher Education has, since 2011, had a clear professional framework, the UK Professional Standards Framework (UKPSF) (Higher Education Academy 2011). This supports ongoing development, encourages creativity and innovation, and defines the professional role of the UK academic. The Academic Development team at Coventry University deliver a Postgraduate Certificate in Academic Practice in Higher Education, which is underpinned by the UKPSF. It seeks to develop staff new to Higher Education as scholarly practitioners, so providing that baseline for continual development and innovation.

Building on this we recognise the importance of course teams as organisational units that can provide a forum for discussion and innovation. Roxa and Martensson (2009) and Roxa *et al*. (2011) have recognised the important link between cohesive teams and quality teaching and learning. Working with university processes, such as course development and annual review, encourages these communities to take a scholarly approach to their practice and continue to innovate. Working with existing processes also acknowledges how academic staff are often time-poor. These existing systems provide a space for interventions from change agents. At Coventry University, these change agents will come from teams such as Academic Development but also digital innovation units such as the Disruptive Media Learning Lab (DMLL) and strategic curriculum projects such as Curriculum 2025. The latter is a project to support development of inclusive curricula that engage in active learning and use of authentic assessments. There will always be flip sides, where course teams have not created an environment for innovation, and in such instances the nature of the interventions will have to reflect this.

Having laid the foundations through encouraging a scholarly approach, supporting ongoing development is essential. This is provided through the provision of faculty-based academic development, which acts as a conduit between academic staff and academic development support, helping to identify local needs, individuals or courses and enabling a responsive level of support. This goes in tandem with a strategic, proactive programme of development activity which seeks to encourage innovation.

The approach Martin outlines is designed to foster an atmosphere in which academics are able to explore new approaches in a comparatively safe environment. As we have outlined, this can be a challenge due to lots of factors, both external and internal, but by providing support to lecturers, the hope is that the established patterns can be challenged, and a culture of continuous change can be introduced. The change agents mentioned have a key role in promoting this new culture and this is reinforced by the way in which staff are recruited for these groups; excellent practitioners are encouraged to take these roles and hence can act as role models for lecturers looking to try 'something new'. There are challenges to this approach. The power of metrics has been explored previously and lecturers are also having to balance increased demands on their time. A recent survey suggested that 83% of lecturers reported that their workload had increased in the last three years (UCU 2017), whilst there have also been reports of a significant increase in cases of problems with the mental health of staff caused by stress. Within this atmosphere, it could be viewed as understandable that staff tend to 'play safe' in their lessons and fall back on what they know rather than try something innovative. The change agents mentioned in our first case study can help mitigate against these problems within a supportive atmosphere, but the central problem of overworking staff is still one that is tricky to resolve.

As well as encouraging staff to try our new approaches, organisations also need to look at institutional procedures that stifle creativity. As mentioned before, when courses are reviewed, or new courses are validated, there are generally a significant number of rules that need to be followed. This bureaucracy-led approach tends to mitigate against freedom of thought (Osborne and Plastrik 1997) and means that staff form approaches more akin to a behaviourist approach as they become used to ensuring that they meet the rules and regulations set down. Many organisations provide guidelines for staff when completing the documentation and again this can limit creativity. It is a hard balance to maintain but what is needed is an approach that reverses the standard way of working, which involves lecturers looking at the rules and regulations and using this as a starting point; instead, the approach should be to work out how rules and regulations can fit the ideas academics have. This would allow far more creativity and encourage those charged with designing new courses to explore different approaches.

Dealing with a lack of knowledge

Turning now to the second barrier, a lack of knowledge. This can be more difficult to overcome. Whilst lecturers are encouraged to keep up to date with their subject knowledge and within the confines of Higher Education are encouraged to research their areas, the pedagogical aspect is rather less well explored. Alongside this, there are many misapprehensions about the introduction of innovative teaching methods. The problems of ensuring that alternative methods can be fitted into quality structures is a key point but whilst this is something that can be addressed using a more enlightened approach, a more general lack of knowledge of either approaches or new methods of teaching can be more challenging to rectify.

One area that typifies this is that of digital literacy. Whilst many organisations are keen to communicate the successes they have had in this area, it is the case that these successes fail to show the full picture. There is a misconception that every member of Generation Z (defined as those born since the mid-1990s) is a 'digital native' (Prensky 2001) and whilst there are some studies that show otherwise (Brown and Czerniewicz 2010; Kirschner and De Bruyckere 2017), universities within the UK are increasingly focusing on finding ways to harness the perceived benefits of embracing new technology and hence appealing to a generation reared on a constant diet of technological innovation.

Whilst it is clear that the increased use of technology in the classroom can have a positive benefit to students (Zhou and Orim 2015), the lack of skills from both students and staff can act as a barrier to full implementation. The dangers of assuming that students have very good digital literacy skills when, in fact, this is not the case, can mean that students are penalised and that assessments are actually testing their aptitude with new technology rather than their subject knowledge. This is something that is particularly important when it comes to the design of assessments.

Despite the problems of implementing new technology, it can have a very positive impact when it embraces factors outside the classroom. With the expansion of students in post-compulsory education, there is a growing concern that not all students can be supported by traditional methods. Kennedy

(1997) identified the issues associated with students who fall into the 'widening participation' categories but there are other groups whose needs need to be addressed. This is especially true when there is a significant event which impacts on students' learning. With innovative and intelligent use of relevant new technologies, support can be maintained, and as we can see from the following case study, enhanced.

Case study 3.2: Supporting students in a time of crisis

Xue Zhou, Assistant Professor, Coventry University

The WeChat group was originally set up to support, both academically and psychologically, the students who were being impacted by COVID-19. Instead of the normal more 'Western' forms of social media (such as Facebook and WhatsApp), we focused on those who used the Chinese social network app, WeChat. This included both Chinese students and Asian students, such as those from Indonesia, Malaysia and India. These Asian students not only have to deal with living many thousands of miles away but they also have language barriers, so they are often not confident in expressing their concerns in their second language. As well as this, we found that there was also a barrier in terms of technology. There are accessibility issues in using Western platforms like Facebook and WhatsApp in the countries these students are from, which means that they have no social connections on these media. They are far more confident with what they know.

Originally, there were eight students who had contacted me with problems and I used these as the starting point, then I asked them to invite their friends – after a week, we had 200 students and four weeks after the start, there were 354. To begin with, just myself and a senior leader from the university were running it, but now another four colleagues are involved. We told the students that we were setting this up so that they could ask me any questions they wanted to. They could pose their questions and we would respond quickly when we had clear answers. We also made sure students were aware of the other university support systems.

We used 'lucky bags', which is a Chinese way to engage people in the group, but in addition to this, students started sharing revision notes and they created their own 'how to' guide for RefWorks. In the first week, we posed academic questions and also discussed cultural differences between the UK and China (for example, why clothes are washed only once a week here and why round tables are rarely used in the UK) to help engage students. We also talked about the pandemic and applied some of the theories to help them make sense of the world.

In the beginning, I was monitoring the group from 7am to 11pm and I answered maybe 30–40 questions every day, but now ... we still receive the same number of questions each day but most of them can be solved by the student colleagues and so I need to do much less. Students have seen the benefits and they have spread the word to other students, not just those from their own course. It's become a community, although some students describe it as a family rather than a group.

I think the group could help with alumni relationships in the future. Students now see Coventry University as a lovely institution, and they recommend it to friends. What is interesting is that if there is an academic question, they will ask the students in the group. Personal questions have also been asked but there is a system for asking those directly to lecturers. These have covered topics as varied and diverse as domestic violence, accommodation concerns and worries about their coursework.

To conclude, why it has been successful is that prior to it being set up, we had nine weeks of face-to-face interactions, which allowed them to build trust in me and so that carries on. The second reason is that they need support and this approach is more efficient than the traditional mechanisms. They are now part of a family and they are not afraid to speak about whatever concerns they might have. This is especially the case because they can speak informally rather than using the formal language of emails. They feel more comfortable in this approach.

Although Xue talks about how the interactions she had before the group started were important, what is noticeable is how digital technology has been used as a vehicle for support rather than an end in itself. The application was selected as being the best fit for students rather than as a means to showcase technology. The students felt supported not because of the technology, but because of the human interaction and the community that was behind it.

Key takeaways

When looking at how we develop new, innovative resources, it is important to look back at the purpose of education and how innovation fits into that knowledge. Although the role of students has changed since the 1992 Further and Higher Education Act, and they are now seen more as consumers than students, the primary purpose of education at these levels remains to further knowledge by engaging and enthusing learners. As with any activity that involves a degree of repetition, the temptation is always to keep doing the same thing without reflecting on what is happening, in other words to fall into a routine.

By looking at both the organisational structures that appear to limit creativity as well as the knowledge and skill of the lecturers, it is possible to disrupt this cycle of repetition and introduce new approaches into the curriculum which aim to engage learners and ensure that what goes on within the organisation stays relevant and up to date.

Inspired by this chapter? Why not try ...

- writing down your daily routine and then looking at ways of changing it
- making sure that every module you teach has one new feature in it
- introducing digital technology that would help engage students in assessment

4 Towards a new approach

TEF Principles this chapter refers to:

Teaching quality: teaching that stimulates and challenges students, and maximises engagement with their studies

Learning environment: resources and activities to support learning and improve retention, progression and attainment

Student outcomes and learning gain: the extent to which all students achieve their educational and professional goals, in particular those from disadvantaged backgrounds

On 11 January 2020, a 61-year-old man from Wuhan Province in China died of a new strain of coronavirus. Whilst sad for his family, this event, at the time, was not considered massively significant. The man had multiple underlying health issues that meant that the virus was able to take hold relatively quickly and coronaviruses had transferred from animals to humans before (most notably with the SARS and MERS outbreaks), and although there was a growing concern that the virus (now coded as COVID-19) did not follow the normal coronavirus pattern of a swift burnout of infection patterns, the impact it would have on everyday life was yet to be grasped around much of the globe. If we fast-forward three months, the world as we know it changed out of all recognition. Words that were not part of our vocabulary such as furloughing, self-isolating and social distancing were now part of the lexicon of everyday life, whilst the world came to grips with the fact that freedom of movement and many other certainties had been replaced with a regimented, isolated, controlled way of living that bore scant resemblance to what had gone before.

Within the education sector, the COVID-19 pandemic has shown us that planning a future strategy for anything is fraught with difficulties. In the space of a few weeks the old certainties, which tended to involve traditional lectures, exams that were sat with a multitude of others in a sports hall and the judicious use of digital technology have been swept away in a stampede towards online, remote learning and new methods of engaging with students. Without the virus creating a vacuum in UK education, it is likely that change would have been incremental rather than the dramatic upheaval that we have witnessed in 2020.

In Chapter 1, we focused on the frames of reference for individuals and how we can encourage lecturers, who are used to a high degree of autonomy, to change their approach. This tends to involve some persuasion from external sources but mostly the change has to come from within the person. What we now know from the pandemic is that whilst micro-changes are always possible with careful planning and organisation, seismic movements often require external factors to encourage the change to happen.

If we accept Lewin's (1947) theory that change management is a three-step process incorporating unfreezing old procedures and assumptions, making the change and then refreezing new procedures and assumptions, we can see that external factors can speed up this process. When it was clear that students could not complete their academic year in its current form, change happened at a breathtakingly fast pace. Initiatives such as switching to online delivery, no-detriment policies and the cancellation of final examinations were brought in quickly and, most importantly, were accepted by academics who previously had resisted changes which would now be viewed as fairly minor.

The contrast between the internal pushes to unfreeze practice and external pushes is clear. The former requires careful planning, well-nuanced arguments about the benefits of the change and also an acceptance by leaders that due to the autonomy that is inherent in the system and a general reluctance to change, the unfreezing process remains problematic. External pushes, however, tend to be more dramatic and have a greater likelihood to encourage the unfreezing stage towards the change phase. It is not simply a binary choice though; returning to the analogy of the education sector as 'the Blob', many external factors have foundered upon a bed of reluctance, antagonism or indifference. So, instead of a simplistic division between internal and external drivers, a more sophisticated approach needs to be used.

To help us begin to understand the external factors that influence change in the sector, we can split them into five separate groups, represented by the mnemonic POET X. These initials represent the following areas:

- Political drivers which encourage the education sector to change
- Organisational drivers which identify how an organisation reacts to external pressures
- Economic drivers which allow organisations to 'chase the money'
- Technological drivers which encourage change and identify if the organisation has the capacity to make the change

The letter X is set apart because it is separate to the other factors. The first four factors are things that can be planned for and in most cases can be addressed before they occur. For example, a change of government and the resultant political upheaval is something that is predictable and the sector has become adept at making sure that it is well versed with any new initiatives and that they have a strategy to address them before they become a reality. This represents good leadership and management and prudent strategic thinking from the organisation can lead to positive changes.

Whilst the presence of one or more of the first four drivers may lead to change, it is not guaranteed. History is littered with initiatives that failed to elicit change. Short-lived policies such as the introduction of A Level Vocational Certificates of Education (AVCEs), 14–19 diplomas and performance-related pay are markers to show that not every external driver is a success. However, when the X driver is present, change becomes inevitable. Whilst the COVID-19 pandemic is an extreme example of this driver, there are others which, although not predicted, have also had a significant impact on the Further and Higher Education sectors.

Political drivers

Political drivers tend to be present in two basic forms: first, in the form of political initiatives that require implementation and, secondly, in the form of political pressure. Whilst the former might be judged more likely to implement change, this is not always the case. Implementation of policy relies on the will at an operational level and that is not always present. An example of this would be the aftermath of the Further and Higher Education Act 1992, which brought incorporation to colleges. The idea that you bring best practice from the private sector to the public sector was a laudable one, but the idea was flawed from the start.

One key problem that implementors of the Act faced was that it was very difficult to identify what was good practice and what was transferable from the private sector (Thompson and Wolstencroft 2018), which meant that newly corporatised colleges were often working in a policy vacuum that was made trickier to handle due to the need to compete with colleges that they had previously collaborated with. The result of the Act was that the sector was engulfed in industrial relations conflicts that lasted three years and although the Further Education landscape did change post-incorporation, the change was not the smooth transition that had been hoped for when the Act was passed.

There are numerous other initiatives that could be cited when looking at change in the education sector. Some, such as the transition of polytechnics to universities, have been accomplished relatively smoothly but there are substantial numbers that have foundered and failed to enthuse the sector. What is interesting is that political pressure often leads to a clearer change. This might well be due to the difficulty of fighting against something without an obvious shape, but it also might be linked to the way in which changing the political landscape has an influence on operational matters.

An example of this might well be the introduction of Ofsted. Whilst the existence of Ofsted remains controversial – indeed, Coffield (2017) described the methods used as invalid, unreliable and unjust – the political will to establish an office looking at standards meant that colleges readjusted their priorities and now have their inspection as a key performance indicator. The examples identified here are just the tip of the iceberg but what they do show is that political drivers can force through change. Ofsted is now well established within the educational framework and incorporation did succeed in the end. The list of failed policies, however, is evidence to show that political drivers alone are rarely strong enough to engender real change.

Organisational drivers

The next set of drivers that can accelerate change can be brought together under the general heading of organisational drivers and these can again impact on whether changes are successful or not. They refer to how organisations react to external pressures and what they prioritise. This then impacts on individuals, as their targets tend to be determined by wider factors.

An example of how this works is when we look at the Teaching Excellence Framework (TEF). When announced, many organisations expressed reservations about both the concept and also the methodology (Barkas *et al.* 2017), but it was how they reacted as institutions that proved most interesting. Many universities planned diligently for its implementation and focused their attention on the key indicators that had been specified. The University of Buckingham, which had the highest overall score in the initial TEF, spent considerable time making sure that their teaching and learning procedures matched those requested in the TEF. The result of this planning was a Gold award.

Other organisations took rather different approaches. Many of the traditional, Russell Group universities were less keen to change and the final results (which gave only eight out of the 21 organisations in this group a Gold rating) reflected this. However, the approach that stressed having confidence in what you do was a notable success in other places, as we see in our first case study. This centres around Middlesbrough College, a large college of further education located in the North East of England, that has 11,000 students and almost 2000 members of staff. The college moved into new buildings in 2008 and a clear focus was put on the culture within the college to ensure that it supported students to take ownership of their learning. The success of this can be shown by the fact that the college was one of the very few to be awarded a Gold rating in the 2018 TEF. The cornerstones for this success are explained by the college's Director of Higher Education.

Case study 4.1: The TEF in Higher Education

Paul Stone, Director of Higher Education, Middlesbrough College

In many ways, the Teaching Excellence Framework was not something that we planned for too far in advance. We would not have been interested if it had only been something that was for show rather than something that reconfirms the quality of our teaching and learning. From the start, we made sure that our approach was to fit the TEF round what we did rather than the other way round.

Because of where we are based, we have a high number of widening partici-pation students in the college and this does impact on our approach. We make sure that we have very strong pastoral support for our students as, for the most part, they are the first generation to go to Higher Education. They are also likely to still be living in the family home and this means that we need to provide study areas for them in the college as well. Every student is different, so what we try to do is offer personalised support and make sure that they are given the skills needed to succeed in Higher Education.

Every student gets 16 hours of contact time at level four and there is a heavy emphasis on face-to-face engagement at this level. Students are given the safety net of a tutor at the lower level but the amount of face-to-face teaching is reduced as students move through the levels. At the heart of everything we put a partnership between staff and students. We have a sabbatical officer who works with us and we try to see what students want from us and work with them to deliver it. To help reinforce this partnership, staff 'hot desk' in a shared staff/student area and they are joined by library and welfare support as well. This gives students a support network and also means that staff and students work closely together.

What we have tried to do is to redefine what teaching is. The focus is very much on learning and so, for example, when we assess sessions it is not about how well they use PowerPoint, it's how they facilitate learning. We also make sure that students realise that the ownership of learning passes to the student as they progress.

This approach is adopted throughout the whole college and this means that the culture is fixed for both staff and students, everyone 'buys into' it and it means that there is consistency. In many ways, the TEF Gold award was a confirmation of what we do rather than the driver of what we do, which is probably as it should be.

As you can see from our first case study, what is noticeable is how the organi-sation used the external driver to very good effect to help validate their standards of teaching and their reputation rather than use it to redefine it.

Another organisational factor that needs to be considered when thinking about change for the future is the individual's ability to change. This is often linked to both the culture of the organisation and the training provided. As we saw with Middlesbrough College, the culture that was engendered in the organisation was one of transformational change. Returning to the previous chapter, this means that an employee's frames of reference are such that they can accept a fluid culture, which makes change that much easier as the unfreezing and refreezing stages are not as deep-rooted (Lewin 1947). The ability of employees to respond is also key. The rush to remote learning pred-icated by the COVID-19 crisis was initially hampered in many organisations by a lack of knowledge on the part of staff about the techniques that might be used to engage students (Zhou and Wolstencroft 2020), which meant that although the will might have been there, employees were not able to implement plans without additional support.

Economic drivers

The relationship between the education sector and the legislative body has always experienced a degree of tension. Nowhere is this exemplified better than in James Callaghan's speech in 1976 at Ruskin College. Colloquially known as the 'Great Debate', it was designed to stimulate discussion about the role of education and in particular the relationship of education to industry. Callaghan asked the question as to whether the primary purpose of education was as a feeder to industry or if there was a wider reason for educating people (Callaghan 1976). A key section of Callaghan's speech explained how the government was spending £6 billion a year on education and this should provide a degree of leverage on the demands of the sector. Whilst the figure has changed significantly, the education budget is £92 billion in 2020, the implication that there will always be a degree of guidance from the government remains.

As explained in Chapter 1, funding for both Further and Higher Education contains a political element and whilst organisations might disagree with the priorities, there is little they can do to prevent government objectives from impacting on what they see as important. The Further Education sector in particular has had to deal with many new initiatives and a key driver for these has been funding. Successive governments have stressed the importance of apprenticeships to the UK economy and so funding has reflected this. Whilst it is not compulsory for colleges to run apprenticeships, if they do not, then they fail to attract the higher levels of funding that those who embrace apprenticeships will benefit from.

Within Higher Education, the economic driver is a powerful force for change. The rapid growth in international students has, in part, been driven by the need to secure additional funding and universities have become adept at prospecting new markets when looking for additional students. Again, returning to Lewin, the refreezing has resulted in many organisations becoming agile in responding to every changing priority.

Technological drivers

The fourth set of drivers that can impact on change and planning for the future are technological drivers, which, as shown in 2020, have the ability to transform education. The digital approaches used are covered in the next chapter but what is of interest here is the speed at which they are adopted when needed. There will always be 'early adopters' of new technology (Rogers 1962) but what has been interesting with many innovations is how quickly they have become the norm rather than something that only a small percentage have embraced.

Kahoot, Padlet and Prezi are now ubiquitous within the classroom and lecture theatre, yet their introduction was not based on a concerted strategy to introduce them; instead, they became common in the organisation as participants realised the benefits they bring to their professional practice. In many ways, this 'what's in it for me?' approach is a stronger driver than when introduced from above, as participants will be more committed to the change if it is driven by themselves. It is also important to think about the availability of technology. Whilst an initial push to use technology can be effective, if the technology is not available this can cause significant problems.

X drivers

The final drivers are those that necessitate immediate change but organisations are not able to plan for. Instead, they require fleet-footed responses and an understanding that refreezing is not always possible when in the middle of a crisis. This can cause uncertainty and worry within the organisation but, with clear leadership, these obstacles can be overcome.

Our second case study looks at how one organisation overcame a unique set of challenges when faced with the COVID-19 virus.

Case study 4.2: COVID-19 – a forced change

Karl Knox, Associate Dean, University of Bedfordshire

We find ourselves in unprecedented times both from an academic perspective and from a student perspective. What follows is a summation of challenges a university has faced, has dealt with, and how both academics and students have managed to maintain a certain amount of educational learning throughout. The impact of the COVID-19 pandemic is not something that will fade away and will in fact affect the educational environment for years to come – changing the face of education in terms of delivery, engagement, management and understanding of what it means to study in an education environment.

The initial 'lockdown' period began on Monday, 23 April 2020. Prior to this point, most academics and students were managing their course and involvement in much the same way that they always had – face to face, blended approach (blogs, forums, etc.), coursework, examinations, seminars and lectures. So, although colleagues were aware of what was intended, and management were preparing both parties with email correspondence, the actual impact, in hindsight, wasn't necessarily internalised or fully understood. The premise to this view is that of colleagues' appreciation for what asynchronous and synchronous teaching actually entailed and that 'moving online' was not just a matter of putting more materials on the Virtual Learning Environment (VLE) and then replicating face-to-face teaching on a digital platform like Skype, Zoom, MS Teams or Blackboard Collaborate.

This shift from face-to-face to asynchronous and synchronous modes of engagement meant colleagues had to rethink the structure, content and pedagogic focus of their unit and subject area. No longer could they be assured of 'getting their message across' in a classroom environment where students were able to then easily follow up with questions. Putting everything 'out there' for all to see suddenly became a hurdle many had not had to address previously – removing that autonomy and control was/is quite scary for both academics and students alike.

Leading up to this point, management took the initiative in terms of supporting this mindset shift by implementing and managing engagement with colleagues virtually. This initially came about by collating online data collection sets.

Electronic forms were used to collect data sets, which in turn allowed operations to continue in virtual space. These included:

- Signing forms – their significance was to identify if colleagues were: (1) 'fit and able to work'; (2) had access to electronic devices to maintain contact and manage their workloads; and (3) had identified any issues that needed further support – internet not working, difficultly in logging onto specific university systems (student data, accounting and or logistical systems).
- Unit information forms – given the university was not aware of how long this may continue, there was a need to change potential in-class test processes, including hand-in dates for assignments, dissertations, etc. Changes to assignment dates and extensions could be done in groups and structured based on data provided to this form by the unit leader.
- Templates and structured announcements were provided to academics to be placed on the front of their VLE unit pages. This ensured consistency for students and assisted colleagues in what was needed – how to efficiently structure their units in the knowledge that all colleagues were following a similar approach. This then created clear expectations and signposting for students and also assisted academic leaders in ensuring that students were being supported and provided with relevant and appropriate data in this fully online environment.

Alongside this initial starting point, training was provided to colleagues with support material, tips on how to manage online units, a discussion community, daily updates (to share best practice) and in essence a refuge (specific area on the VLE – test areas) for them to feel comfortable in managing the changes that were occurring, to fit resources and ask questions. Much of the support was an attempt to reassure academics that this is just how it is (we can do this) and how we now have to operate for the immediate future; as opposed to some form of monitoring systems akin to an endless observation process. In the online environment, everything one does is open and accessible for all to see (i.e. peers, management and students). Addressing this has taken the form of reassuring and supporting colleagues with daily updates, portfolio meetings and an approach from academic leaders to contact all academics throughout the week individually that has resulted in a shared perspective that 'we are all in this together and will manage this together'. To date, recognition of and changes made include:

- A movement of in-class tests to an online format for submission, without changing content; exams and management of them being rescheduled to later in the academic calendar but still allowing progression boards to occur
- Support for group changes to unit assessment, approved and acknowledged to maintain the quality standards
- Dissertations – primary and secondary research, stage of dissertation and a differentiation as to whether this is undergraduate or postgraduate – impacts on extensions – which have been generously applied
- All assessments that were to occur after 23 March automatically received a two-week extension to allow alternative arrangements and processes to be implemented
- Daily updates from management and a weekly reflection from the Dean
- Much of the guidance has been aimed at academics working more asynchronously, directing students and then having concentrated synchronous sessions with, what seems to be better, more structured participation. One colleague referred this to me as a 'throwback to the days when students came to class having read the material and being prepared'.
- The use of data sets to support academics also allowed clear engagement with visiting lecturers/hourly paid lecturers ensuring that all parties delivering were supported.

Feedback, to date, from academics on the process of online delivery is based somewhat on their starting point in terms of using different mediums for engagement with students, the speed at which this change has been implemented and the acceptance of students to maintain contact and involvement.

Academics have acknowledged:

- In some cases, more students are turning up to specific synchronous sessions, so a feeling of better engagement – how long for remains to be seen
- A complete feeling of being 'wiped out' at the end of the day with a constant need to be at their desk or computer – moving forward, more guidance is needed
- An opportunity to reflect more thoroughly upon their units and the content of the unit
- A recognition of their lack of IT literacy compared with the needs of students and ability to work in an online environment completely
- The support from 'learning support' and other service departments throughout the university has been enlightening – on par with a 'war effort' mentality

Students have acknowledged:

- A real difference in how they think about their studies and the importance to have access to their tutors
- A completely different approach by some tutors has changed the way students interact and enjoy the subject area
- An appreciation of the amount of extra support academics are providing and the emphasis on maintaining normality in trying times

Going forward, the impact of the COVID-19 pandemic will ultimately change how educational institutions operate. The need to completely run in a face-to-face format will be replaced with a truly integrated, blended learning approach and structure, not one that has until now been seen by some as 'paying lip service' to the changes that are needed.

As you can see from this case study, the organisation reacted in a clear and decisive manner when faced with the problem. The key driver came from the leadership team who provided guidance and direction where needed. Because of this clear guidance, members of staff followed instructions, and this meant that the change phase was completed all together rather than everyone doing their own individual things. There are, of course, problems with this, as such an autocratic style of leadership is not always best suited to education institutions and, if used in other circumstances, could cause conflict but, as a short-term strategy, it is highly effective.

Of course, COVID-19 is not the only X driver faced by education, but it does give a clear insight into the approach needed and also that when these factors come along, it is possible to make both substantial and major changes to the organisation in a short space of time, whereas if not present these changes would be resisted.

Key takeaways

Returning to the opening of this chapter, what we saw in 2020 is something that could hardly have been envisaged, but it has demonstrated how change can be enacted to ensure that education continues to serve the needs of the students. Whilst normally change requires an intellectual rationale and slow, increment progress, it is possible to identify certain factors that, when present, can facilitate rapid change.

The problem with some of these changes is that it is not always possible to prepare for them and so what happens is that organisations have to react rather than plan. The situation created when either an X driver or, to a lesser extent, a different type of driver is present, can best be described as akin to a vacuum. Given that nature abhors a vacuum, there is a rush to fill it and so significant changes are possible in a relatively short period of time.

Inspired by this chapter? Why not try ...

- *identifying factors affecting your organisation in each of the POET X categories, trying to work out whether you will be able to plan for these events*
- *scenario planning for X driver events – it may not be possible, but it is a good exercise to get you thinking about whether you are ready*
- *looking at the technological part – that is something that can often hold organisations back so maybe prepare for it*

Part 2

Learning Environment

5 Digital learning

TEF Principles this chapter refers to:

Teaching quality: teaching that stimulates and challenges students, and maximises engagement with their studies

Learning environment: resources and activities to support learning and improve retention, progression and attainment

Back in the early 2010s, the educational world was full of stories and reports about how Mass Open Online Courses (MOOCs) were going to transform, if not revolutionise education, in particular the university sector. The new MOOC platforms (such as Coursera, edX, Udacity) were going to challenge traditional university education and force a fundamental rethink of how we conceive of a Higher Education learning experience. The zeitgeist was captured in the title of a widely commented on paper from the Institute of Public Policy Research (IPPR), 'An avalanche is coming' (Barber *et al.* 2013). At the centre of the anticipated avalanche was the rapid development of digital learning technology and environments. Nearly ten years on though there were clearly some indications of movement, some shifts in the underlying ground, but as yet universities and the core, timeless structures of Higher Education – such as three- or four-year undergraduate degrees, lectures, nine-month 'years' and paper-based traditional exams – had not been swept away. However, this may be about to change in a rapid and previously unforeseen way. One of the unintended consequences of the COVID-19 pandemic is that it might finally trigger the avalanche predicted by the Institute for Public Policy Research (IPPR). Even before COVID-19 hit, it was clear that digital technologies were becoming ever more pervasive. One of the many consequences of this has been that universities and colleges have had to move to using digital learning environments if they are to maintain their core service of delivering and assessing their courses. We shall return to this issue at the end of the chapter.

Many of the chapters in this book reference and highlight applications of digital technology across a wide range of educational practice. It did feel though that pre-COVID-19 we were still a long way from recognising and embracing the full impact of digital technology and the inherent potential to transform learning it promises.

As highlighted above, given that digital tools, environments, resources, support and learning approaches will feature in many guises throughout the forthcoming chapters, the purpose of this chapter is to focus on the educators: how the widespread adoption of digital technology might change, or at least has the potential to change, our professional practice as educators. The futurologist and sci-fi writer Arthur C. Clarke made many perceptive comments over the course of his long life; one of the more often quoted is directly relevant to our discussion: 'any teacher that can be replaced by a machine should be' (cited in McAleer 2013). This raises the follow-on question of what can a teacher do that a machine (taken as a proxy for the digital learning environment) cannot? As we move into the next phase of digital development, which is likely to be dominated by developments in artificial intelligence (AI) and big data, this question becomes even more pressing.

The rest of this chapter will focus on three potential ways in which educators can take advantage of the opportunities offered by digital technology whilst still remaining central to supporting a student's learning.

1   Educators as curators of knowledge
2   Educators as facilitators of learning
3   Educators as adjudicators of standards

Digital learning environments should be driven by the pedagogy, not the other way around; when done effectively, it can make learning relevant, engaging and even more fun!

However, it is important also to recognise why, pre-COVID-19, the avalanche hadn't quite happened. Many of the excellent case studies included in this book, which use digital technologies, tend to be by their very nature at module level. One issue that often arises is around the scalability and sustainability of these innovative approaches. Can the innovations be scaled up beyond a module? Can they be embedded in a module/course pedagogy so that they do not rely on a single or small group of enthusiastic advocates? Even where there are more ambitious course or institutional strategies, however, 'Many educational innovations using technology have thrilled with potential and disappointed in reality' (Oldfield *et al.* 2016). The chapter concludes with some thoughts on why this might be the case. What are the potential blockers that have been holding the avalanche back for the moment?

Curators of knowledge

One of the common complaints heard from colleagues is that students don't pay attention in formal lectures, '… they're always messing with their phones'. The assumption is that they are chatting with their friends, checking the latest feeds about their football team or any number of potential activities within the capacity of a smart phone. One response to this moan is to challenge the assumption about what students are looking at on their phones. What if they are not communicating with friends or looking at football news at all? What if they are checking what is being presented in the lecture is actually correct? Take, for example, one of the staples of any business course, a framework usually referred to as 'Porter's five forces' (Porter 1979) – any student who has ever done a strategy or marketing module will be familiar with the framework. An internet search on 'Porter's five forces' leads to dozens of explanations of the framework, including impressive full-colour charts, animated charts, talking heads, slides and more besides. What you may also find is a YouTube video of the Harvard Professor, Michael Porter, explaining the principles behind the framework that bears his name (Porter 2008). To go back to the original point: if an academic complains about a student messing with their phone whilst they are explaining 'Porter's five forces' in a lecture, what the student might actually be doing is seeing what Michael Porter himself says about his framework.

We live in a world, and more importantly, the majority of our students have grown up in a world, where information is pervasive. We have instant, boundary-less, free access to digitised information. A simple internet search will provide answers and information on just about anything to the extent that there is actually a term (and even competitions) to find searches which only lead to one hit – a googlewhack. This new instant information-rich world has a number of implications in terms of learning environments and offers the potential to rethink the role of ourselves as educators.

Those of us of a certain age will remember a popular series of adverts for the Martini range of drinks run in the 1980s and 1990s with the strapline, 'Anytime, anyplace, anywhere' (Leech 2014). The pervasive digital environment we now live in has the potential to do the same thing for learning. Access to information and data and the process of teaching are no longer fixed to a specified time or place, be it a lecture theatre, classroom, library or home study. Like the Martini motto, it has the potential to be available 'anytime, anyplace, anywhere'.

The second implication of the digital environment is the idea that learning can be 'just in time' rather than 'just in case'. The Scottish comedian Billy Connolly used to include in his stage show a routine based on the futility of being taught algebra in school: 'Why should I learn algebra when I've no intention of ever going there?' (Connolly 2009). He would go on to say, 'I have never used algebra since the day I left school ... never seen anybody using it ... never heard of anyone who used it' (this is a slightly censored version!). What Connolly is actually ranting against is an example of 'just in case' learning – he's been force taught algebra just in case he is one of the very small minority of people who go on to university and study a maths-based subject. If one of the large majority did actually find that they needed to use algebra later in life, they could instantly access through their smart phone any number of available online resources to help and engage in some 'just in time' learning.

Facilitators of learning

So how does the 'anytime, anyplace, anywhere' learning environment potentially impact on the role of educational practitioner? To go back to Arthur C. Clarke's comment, what is it that a machine cannot do that a teacher can? Good teaching, in whatever context, has always reflected a balance between the transmission of knowledge and the active application and engagement with knowledge by the students. However instant, boundaryless and free access to information enables a decisive shift in a teacher's role away from the delivery of knowledge to a guiding and curating role. It allows us to move away from viewing our primary role as being the transmitters of knowledge to one where we are more curators of knowledge – a move from 'being the sage on the stage to guide on the side' (King 1993).

In the early 2000s, Prensky coined the term 'digital natives' (2001) to describe the generation of students that were growing up in a world where, not only information was increasingly instant and free, but social relationship were becoming governed by social media. Nearly 20 years on, you really need to be approaching your 40s to recall a pre-internet, pre-mobile phone world. However, there is a body of evidence (Beetham *et al.* 2009) to suggest that the 'digital native' student still needs guidance and support to transfer the digital skills they develop in their everyday life being put to good effect to support their learning. The need to develop digital literacy skills to support learning is just as relevant for students as it is for their teachers.

Another role for the educator is to ensure that they are supporting the 'any-time, anyplace, anywhere' opportunities offered by a digital learning environment through the use of digital learning tools and virtual learning environment (VLE) platforms. Indeed, digital learning platforms and tools increasingly offer the potential to develop new approaches to pedagogy such as flipped learning, peer-to-peer learning and even the co-creation of knowledge. It is important, however, to ensure that whatever the method being used, it is the pedagogy that is driving delivery and not the technology (Sharples 2019). It is still the case that sometimes a pen and piece of paper will do!

Our first case study considers how one university has tried to drive forward innovative change to pedagogy through the establishment of an experimental learning unit.

Case study 5.1: Disruptive Media Learning Lab

Coventry University (dmll.org.uk)

In the context of globally networked societies and accelerated social and technological change, the educational landscape is going through a period of significant transformation where the role of educators, content, infrastructures and institutions in supporting learning need to be reimagined. How can Higher Education respond to this challenge and transform teaching, learning and assessment practices in an agile, positive and meaningful way?

Responding to that challenge, Coventry University established the Disruptive Media Learning Lab (DMLL) in 2014 as an experimental unit specifically devoted to driving forward innovation in teaching, learning, assessment and scholarly practice, so that the university can re-model its own approaches through testing and mainstreaming innovative ideas. A shift from traditional didactic approaches to more student-centric, engaging, active and social learning experiences through a number of new models and mindsets has been the key focus on the Lab since its inception.

Development

- DMLL was initially launched as a three-year pilot and at the end of that period it was reconfigured and consolidated as a permanent unit of Coventry University Group. As a result of this reconfiguration, three key thematic areas emerged: Digital Fluency and Networked Learning, Playful and Gameful Learning, and Flipped Learning.
- DMLL instigates and supports different kinds of initiatives and projects. Some of them have been co-designed with staff working in discipline-specific contexts, while others are aimed at the whole CU community.
- Even though the key priority of DMLL is to foster educational innovation within Coventry University Group, its impact has extended far beyond thanks to the open education ethos underpinning its activity and a wide range of international partnerships. The work with internal stakeholders and external partners mutually benefits and reinforces each other, contributing to the formation of a virtuous circle on innovation.

Implementation

DMLL has supported the implementation of educational innovations of different kinds through an extensive portfolio of projects and broader initiatives. The *GameChangers* programme exemplifies the way DMLL operates and illustrates the diversity and reach of the educational innovations it facilitates. Fostering open learning practices through the development of an empathic and holistic approach to co-creating playful and gameful educational resources, it has empowered educators on an international scale to creatively innovate their own teaching practices. Building on established research into game-based pedagogies, several open-source models for informing the design of game-based learning resources (including an online open course) have been simplified for rapid acceptance and adoption amongst educators, and have been put into practice at the university and beyond (internationally).

These models have informed a number of externally funded projects (value of over £9 million since 2015). Most recently, in 2019–20, DMLL has been awarded over £1.5 million through the Global Challenges Research Fund to further expand the impact of empathic game-based learning approaches to South East Asia, building on the work it has already done in Borneo (Malaysia) to adopt the *GameChangers* approach. The programme has won numerous awards, including the Gamification Award for Research 2018 for its pioneering work in escape game methodology for education, the Gamification Award for Education and Learning 2019 for its international impact, and the Gamification Award for Software 2019 for innovative game-based learning authoring funded through H2020, which was coordinated by the *GameChangers* team.

An agile and responsive research–development–practice cycle underpins the DMLL approach to fostering educational innovation. This is demonstrated by the implementation of new practices and methods across the university, which has also received traction internationally, producing both social and economic impact. An empathic and inclusive approach to co-creation and co-production has been key to expanding the impact of DMLL. In this respect, *GameChangers* innovates the way play and games are used in education through a focus on literacy in game design and game making. This emphasis on empowering and upskilling educators towards mobilising learners and transforming education aligns with UNESCO's focus on teachers as the key instruments for addressing all the targets of the UN's sustainable development goal 4 on equitable, inclusive quality education. The same approach has also seen gamified learning piloted in Europe and beyond (10 countries, engaging with over 6000 educators and learners), which has achieved 84% satisfaction in terms of educational experience. Educators were empowered to innovate through the creation of their own gamified learning experiences.

Other DMLL projects and initiatives include:

- Work on the potential of the open web for teaching and learning, as exemplified by Coventry.domains, a Domain of One's Own initiative that provides staff and students with web-hosting space and a (sub)domain name enabling them to experiment with web-publishing systems and other web technologies while taking more control over their online presence. The new Wikimedian in Residence Programme has been recently launched to explore also the opportunities for learning through active and critical engagement with Wikipedia.
- EduHack.eu: an EU-funded project aimed at building digital education capacity and exploring the potential of hackathons as a format for educational innovation and academic development in Higher Education.
- Experimental Add+Vantage Modules: DMLL has offered a number of optional modules with the aim of testing approaches and developing learning resources relating to some other initiatives.
- Student Activators: students from any course can join the DMLL team for a period of time to gain paid work experience in a number of areas.
- Digital Leaders: an extra-curricular programme offering students from any course the opportunity to develop Digital Fluency through planning and delivering activities aimed at raising awareness among peers of relevant topics they choose to explore with the guidance of DMLL staff.
- Online Welcome Facilitator training of the University Induction programme.

Feedback from teachers and students

The following feedback summarises the role DMLL plays in fostering and helping share innovative practices:

"As much as ideas, though, it's been good to get people's comments on what I'm doing and to know that other people are thinking of similar ideas and that I'm not just doing something alone, at a tangent to the direction of the university"

And this other piece of feedback illustrates how DMLL has a positive impact on students:

"By working for DMLL, I am still able to learn whilst working very professionally in a creative environment. I am always free to have my opinion as a Graphic

Designer and am always included. DMLL has really helped me find my place in the design industry which I am very thankful for"

DMLL initiatives such as *GameChangers* are regularly evaluated through both quantitative and qualitative indicators (Arnab *et al.* 2019a, 2019b).

Impact of the DMLL

DMLL has evolved and strived to reposition and reconfigure education at Coventry University within the rapidly changing technological, social, economic and political contexts shaping the learning landscape. The Lab has successfully created a space and culture of innovation in which collaboration and interdisciplinarity are the key attributes of the research, development and practice outcomes of pathfinder and exploratory projects. DMLL focuses on how both mainstream and innovative approaches and technologies are explored, repurposed and remixed towards conceptualising a more hybrid and open approach to teaching and learning, in order to meet a wide range of learner needs.

Core to the success of the Lab is the distinctive inter-connected cycle which directly links internal innovation together with external partners. These are a selection of key achievements:

1 Supported more than 50 projects and initiatives.
2 Engaged with more than 3000 students, 1000 staff members and 30 courses across the CU Group.
3 More than 100 international partners in countries including Brazil, Germany, Romania, Greece, Portugal, France, Spain, Canada, USA, Italy, Chile, Norway, Finland, Morocco, Palestine, Jordan and Egypt.

As an example, through the *GameChangers* programme, a module on playful design has been embedded as part of the formal curriculum. Based on the four cohorts of students from the different faculties, we achieved an average of over 90% satisfaction in the MEQs (Module Evaluation Questionnaires). Based on the research and evaluation carried out on the emphatic approach for developing our students into emotionally intelligent and creative innovators, the students discovered the value of non-disciplinary specific competencies such as empathy (socio-emotional), creativity, communication and team working. They have also discovered the importance of arts and humanities in STEM disciplines, which would enhance their understanding of their own specific disciplines. Through our work internationally, such as the adaptation of *GameChangers* in Malaysia, teachers in remote parts of Borneo have been upskilled with *GameChangers'* empathic game literacy approach, where during the adaptation, they have so far created over 20 game-based learning resources that are being used in schools. They have also developed guidelines for other teachers.

Adjudicator of standards

There is however one aspect of an educator's role that cannot change. The teacher needs to assess students work, they have to judge how well the student has grasped and/or used the concepts and ideas that make up the course curriculum. Having said that though, as digital technology continues to develop so the potential for digitising assessment becomes ever greater. The recently published Joint Information Systems Committee (JISC) report on assessment (JISC 2020) sets out five principles around which, they suggest, future assessment should be based. Not surprisingly, given the source, the JISC authors make a strong case that the five principles are best supported by the adoption of a fully digitised approach to assessment.

1 Authenticity – used creatively, digitised assessment allows for a greater range of authentic assessment strategies to be developed.
2 Accessibility – digitised assessment facilitates the delivery of assessments in a variety of forms to suit the needs of the learners.
3 Appropriately automated – certain forms of assessment lend themselves to computer-assisted marking, which benefits both the teacher (less time marking) and the student (instant feedback).
4 Continuous – digitised assessment supports the building of assessment into the curriculum in an integrated manner that embeds assessment as a key aspect of the learning process.
5 Secure – the use of digital submission, marking and feedback provides a more secure assessment environment both from the academic integrity and administrative perspectives.

Technology to support assessment is already widely used through plagiarism software, electronic submission of coursework, online quizzes through VLEs and many digital assessment tools that are currently available. What is far less common is the use by institutions of a holistic approach to digitising assessment, including examinations. The exception is in Scandinavia where the digitising of exams is becoming more common, particularly in Denmark where the Danish government's digital strategy for the economy includes the digitisation of all assessments in schools and universities.

Within the UK a number of universities are also looking at adopting digital assessment. In our second case study, Muhammad reflects on his experience whilst at Brunel University in leading the introduction of the digital assessment platform WISEflow across the Business School.

Case study 5.2: WISEflow – a university-wide digital assessment platform

Muhammad Kamal, Coventry University (formerly of Brunel University)

Universities focus on developing their students for successful careers (for better employability opportunities), i.e. developing them for a digital future. In this case, innovative technological solutions can facilitate universities to meaningfully evaluate students' capabilities, skills and aptitudes that are necessary to thrive in the global competitive world of work. With this salient outlook, will the universities still focus on traditional summative and examination assessment methods or want to move to the digital versions of pen and paper assessment? In line with the latter, Brunel University London decided upon digitalising their assessments and online examination. WISEflow is Brunel University London's digital assessment platform – this decision was carried out after extensive soft market assessment of different digital assessment vendors. Brunel University London went from proof of principle in 2015–16 to now university-wide adoption of WISEflow in 2019–20 across all three colleges (College of Business Arts and Social Sciences [CBASS], College of Engineering, Design and Physical Sciences [CEDPS] and College of Health and Life Sciences [CHLS]). Before moving to university-wide adoption, in the first two years, extensive piloting was undertaken to ensure all issues related to its adoption and implementation are identified including preferences of academics and feedback from students.

As stated above, WISEflow was adopted for mainly summative coursework submission across different departments (e.g. individual module-related coursework, undergraduate final-year projects, and MSc and MBA dissertations) and examinations (e.g. onsite, time-limited, and monitored assessments), with some departments also using it for digital Bring Your Own Device (BYOD) examinations.

For example, considering the example of Brunel Business School (BBS) where I championed the adoption of WISEflow, a gradual approach was undertaken. In the first instant, two modules (100% coursework based) were piloted at BBS. This pilot provided a significant alternative to assess students more effectively and efficiently. After a successful trial on the first two modules, two additional modules (100% exam based) were piloted, with a small cohort. The module leaders for these two exam-based modules were provided training on the use of WISEflow and how to monitor the examination process. The second trial was also successful, well supported by the module leaders, and received positive feedback from the students taking an exam using a digital platform. Other benefits included students not able to cheat, since when WISEflow is installed onto any system, it disables other features of the device. However, in order to respect individual learners and the diverse learning communities within BBS, some of the students were allowed to sit their exam using the conventional method, as they were able to quickly write as supposed to typing using the keyboards. With these two successful pilots, BBS moved on to assessment of modules with bigger cohorts. The module used was undergraduate dissertations (with well over 400 students). To go ahead with this big move, the necessary training was provided to all the academics (30+) involved in supervising and marking dissertations. Students were also offered training on how to submit their coursework and appear in exams. The pilot module was also successful – all submissions were submitted successfully. However, where successes were acknowledged, several issues were also noted. For example, from the point of view of people-related issues, there was some resistance from a few colleagues on the use of a new platform who persisted with Blackboard Learn, Brunel's VLE. Despite several training sessions, a few academics remained unwilling to use WISEflow. From the point of view of technical issues, WISEflow was not able to support students in writing complicated mathematical formulas (e.g. ratios, econometric formulas, etc.), or provide technical support for students while appearing for exams, etc.

Thus far, Brunel University London has gone from 600+ coursework submissions in 2015–16 to well over 50,000 in 2019–20, whilst the number of exams went from one module for around 150 students to 80+ exams for well over 2700 students in the same period. The reason for adopting WISEflow was to enhance the overall assessment process across the university, using rubrics and a standardised marking scheme – all to provide more consistent feedback, enhancing student experience and impacting their behaviour in learning different technologies. Now that WISEflow is adopted university-wide, Brunel University London has dedicated web links to offer support and resources to module leaders, flow managers in the taught programme office, students, markers, moderators and external examiners. For several years, Brunel University London has been using Blackboard Learn. All summative submissions were uploaded through Blackboard Learn and where possible using Turnitin independently for plagiarism checks. The WISEflow platform offers embedded plagiarism detection software (i.e. URKUND) that supports the generation of a similarity report once the students submit their piece of work. This is another great feature of WISEflow (although embedded within WISEflow) that enabled the markers to view the scripts as well as the similarity report at the same time and offer feedback accordingly.

As an educationist, I understand the significance of assessment and more specifically assessment through a digital platform. Digital transformation is a momentous task, but universities must move away from their traditional summative and formative assessment methods and focus on digital versions of pen and paper assessment. Considering the people- and technical-related issues and challenges, which can be resolved, I would therefore recommend other universities to take a gradual approach to adopting digital assessment platforms. All this is possible, but subject to providing in-depth training to academics, consulting staff whilst deciding on such a big move, providing detailed learning resources, and learning from the best practices of using WISEflow from other education institutions. Although innovative practice of digital assessment is within reach of all universities, for the move towards digitalisation to occur, decision-makers in universities need to drive this forward. Based on the huge increase in digital submissions over the years at Brunel University London, it appears that there is now a rich source of data. This data, in the future, can explicitly show how the assessments can be used for learning. In general, the future of assessment in universities is not reusing outdated assessment methods, but empowering universities with digital assessment or e-assessment.

In summary, several positive aspects and negative issues related to people and technology were reported:

People-related outcomes

Positives:

- Greater willingness and support from top management for WISEflow adoption and implementation university-wide

- Greater engagement by tech-savvy staff
- Enhancing assessment practice for staff and students

Negatives:

- Lack of consultation with academics and admin staff on the decision to move to WISEflow adoption, university-wide
- Lack of will and resistance to change to new assessment platform and no constant support from the WISEflow technical team
- Staff not ready – despite undertaking several training sessions

Technology-related outcomes

Positives:

- Transforming the overall assessment process, i.e. taking exam anytime and anywhere
- Real-time monitoring of examination process
- Marking using in-built rubric is more structured and efficient

Negatives:

- Students see the feedback but not the marks – perhaps a technical glitch, but resulting in panic among staff and students
- With more than one marker, there is no anonymity, i.e. first marker can view the marks and feedback of the second marker, and vice versa, mainly for undergraduate final-year projects (where there are two anonymous markers)
- Lack of support for writing complicated mathematical formulas, e.g. ratios, econometric formulas

So, what has been holding the avalanche back?

The previous three sections have shown that, despite the increasing capabilities and potential offered by a digital learning environment, there are still things an academic can do that a machine cannot. This, however, does not answer the other question posed at the start of the chapter about why much of the development in the use of digital learning environment was, pre-COVID-19, still largely driven by pockets of enthusiastic adopters. What was holding back the avalanche that was so confidently predicted nearly 10 years ago?

The answers are not hard to find, and I'm sure many of the authors of the case studies in this book would recognise the blocks on innovation discussed below.

Support systems and processes

The use of VLEs is almost universal across education, although in terms of support for teaching and learning they are most commonly used as repositories of learning support resources. However, once a VLE is used to facilitate credited, assessed coursework, amendments need to be made to the supporting administrative and quality assurance processes to maintain standards and ensure the validity of the assessment process. Many colleges and universities have moved to online submission of coursework and made the necessary adjustments to the regulatory processes. The move to a fully digitised holistic assessment including examinations, some of which may be taken remotely, is a new dynamic. The advantages in terms of security (as noted in the JISC report) plus cost savings (paper, storage, administrative support) are clear – however, the need to fundamentally change all the processes and quality assurance procedures is a significant block.

Motivation to change: 'We've always done it this way and it works'

Change can be unsettling. When faced with an experienced colleague, who is an exceptional teacher and receives excellent student feedback but takes a traditional pedagogic approach, it can be very challenging to convince them of the need to change. Perhaps we shouldn't. However, for most of our colleagues there is a need to nudge them in the direction of developing their professional practice to take advantage of the opportunities offered by a digital learning environment. Economic history is full of examples of long forgotten companies, even whole industries, who took the attitude 'We've always done it this way and it works!'

Digital competence

Perhaps closely linked to the previous block is the issue of digital literacy. A refusal by a colleague to change their professional practice may actually hide a lack of confidence in their digital literacy rather than an unwillingness to change. In addition, despite the term 'digital native' commonly used to describe Millennials and Gen Zers, it is wrong to assume that this applies to all our students. Many of our students who come from under-developed parts of the world, or less privileged backgrounds (or both), may have the same digital literacy needs as some of our colleagues.

Resource implications

In a university context, a mass lecture with over 400 students being taught at the same time is very resource efficient, both in terms of physical space and staff time. The move to a more flexible pedagogical approach supported by a digitised learning environment is a costly option. Not only do you need to invest in developing the technical aspects of creating an online learning space, you also need to factor in the physical space costs and your staffing resources.

The common theme underlying each of these blocks, also highlighted in Muhammad's case study on digital assessment, is the need for clear direction, support and commitment from senior management to make the change happen. The other key management issue, highlighted by Muhammad's experience at Brunel, is the need to have properly structured and supported staff development, for both academic and professional service staff. The recent COVID-19 pandemic has, however, focused minds and in many institutions has forced senior management to look closely at their institutional capability to offer online teaching and assessment. To use Lewin's (1947) framework referred to in Chapter 4, we are currently in a forced 'change' part of the three-stage change process. COVID-19 appears to be forcing an unfreezing from some of the timeless practices highlighted at the start of this chapter. What will be interesting is how institutions refreeze post COVID-19 – could this finally lead to the avalanche happening?

Before closing this chapter, it is important to consider some potentially negative impacts of moving to an 'anytime, anyplace, anywhere' learning environment. Closely related to student digital competency referred to above is the very real worry about the equity of access to technology, particularly in the Further Education context. It is simply wrong to assume that all students have access to smart phones, tablets, laptops and WiFi away from the college. Finally, given the increasing concern around student health and wellbeing, we do not have much evidence on how moving to a more digital learning environment impacts on a student's mental health.

Key takeaways

The one big question hanging over the area of digital learning is the potential impact of COVID-19. The forced change that many universities and colleges have had to make to their learning and assessment practices has accelerated the rate of change in the adoption of digital learning. The question is, when the refreeze happens will there have been a change in behaviour and attitudes towards digital learning or will there be a drift back to the old practices?

Moving to a more digitally enhanced learning environment can be both daunting and intimidating for both educators and students. The effective use of a digital learning environment implies that the educator's role needs to change from an essentially 'teacher' transmission of knowledge role to a curator and facilitator of learning. The challenge for students is the need to increasingly become active, engaged learners not passive receivers of information, plus there is a danger of the digital divide widening between those with access to technology and those without.

Underpinning both of the issues raised above, as demonstrated in the two case studies, is the need for comprehensive, structured and supportive academic, professional service and student development.

Inspired by this chapter? Why not try ...

- *next time you need to introduce a new concept/model, stepping back and letting the students search out resources and explore the concept/model for themselves*
- *searching out the digital open resources which may be available to support your course*
- *using one of the many software packages (Tophat, Padlet, Socrative) on the market to make your lecture more interactive*

6 Engaging with the outside world

TEF Principles this chapter refers to:

Learning environment: resources and activities to support learning and improve retention, progression and attainment

"No man is an island entire of itself; every man is a piece of the continent, a part of the main"

– Donne 1624

This truism certainly applies to our students. This chapter considers two aspects of how a student's engagement with the world outside of the college or university campus can impact on their on-course educational experiences. On a local level a student, and their institution, exists within a local community that can be a source of both mutual benefit but also tension. On a broader level, students have traditionally engaged with wider societal issues. At the moment, one of the most pressing societal issues is sustainability and how we should be responding to the challenges this presents. The two case studies presented in this chapter reflect these two aspects of how students can engage with the outside world and how the outcome can be mutually beneficial, often in unanticipated ways.

Town versus gown

Picture the following scene, which could be found in any number of cities and towns on a daily basis – a pub in the centre of the town with students enjoying a few afternoon drinks. Unfortunately, a couple of the students feel that their drinks are not up to the usual standard and go to complain to the landlord. The landlord takes exception to the complaint about the quality of his product and an argument breaks out between him and the students. What happens next is perhaps less common, but not unknown, as the quarrel quickly deteriorates into a mass brawl between the students' friends and the locals in the pub. Thankfully what happens next is even less common, as the pub brawl escalates into a full-blown three-day riot between the city's students and the townsfolk leaving nearly a hundred people dead. This event actually took place in Oxford in 1355 in what became known as the St. Scholastica's Day riot (Mallet 1924). This rather extreme example of 'town vs. gown' rivalry illustrates the long-standing, often fractious, nature of the relationship between a university and its surrounding communities. Similar tensions exist in many of today's university towns, for example around the issue of student housing, with whole neighbourhoods becoming in effect student ghettoes, to the annoyance of the remaining local residents. Fortunately, none so far have led to a repeat of the St. Scholastica's Day riot!

However, we cannot get away from the fact that universities and colleges are an integral part of their local communities, even more so for those based in towns rather than out-of-town campuses. As already noted, the impact on a town or city of the needs of a large transient student population requiring accommodation can be significant, not only on community relations but also on the local housing economy. In Newcastle and Exeter, for example, roughly one in 15 properties in those cities are student accommodation (Holland 2018). Apart from the local housing market, universities and colleges also have significant impacts on a town or city's local service economies, particularly in the medium-sized and smaller cities such as Newcastle, Coventry, Exeter and Leicester. Local food outlets, personal services, taxis and the gig-economy in these cities are largely driven by student demand. Finally, universities and colleges are also significant as employers, often being counted amongst the largest companies by headcount in many local economies. The mutual interdependence outlined above of a university and its local community was recognised when, in May 2019, over 50 universities signed up to the Civic University Agreement pledging themselves to: '... put the economy and quality of life in their home towns and cities at the top of their list of priorities' (UPP Foundation 2019).

There has been a long-standing tradition at many universities and colleges of students engaging with the local community through, for example, the fund-raising activities associated with Rag Weeks or undertaking community-based projects. However, what is perhaps less common is a student engaging in a conscious way with the world outside the campus as part of their learning. A phrase often heard in the classroom is 'in the real world'. Should we, as educationalists, be making better use of the real-world community outside the university as a learning environment either to support a student's main course or as a valuable learning experience to enrich their studies?

Many universities, colleges and their associated Student Unions offer opportunities for students to volunteer in their local communities. However, what is less common is for these schemes to be embedded within courses in the form of credit-bearing modules. The case study below concerns a volunteering scheme run by the Student Union at Coventry University (CUSU), which is part of the university's Add+vantage scheme. Add+vantage modules are compulsory ten-credit modules embedded in each stage of the majority of undergraduate courses aimed at providing opportunities for students to enhance their employ-ability. The case study considers students on an Add+vantage module engag-ing in local schools in a way that not only benefits the school, but allows the student to gain academic credit.

Case study 6.1: Students volunteering and some unintended consequences

Phil Pilkington, formerly Coventry University Student's Union

Coventry University Students' Union (CUSU) initiated student volunteering in Coventry and Warwickshire with the financial support of Millennium Volun-teers (MV) and the HEFCE-funded Active Community Fund (ACF), in tandem with the Add+Vantage Modules introduced to develop employability skills for undergraduates at all levels of study.

The volunteering ranged from befriending people with mental health problems, elderly and isolated Asian women, local wildlife trusts and other local commu-nity groups. The largest group of student volunteers from the MV beginnings, however, were those placed within local primary, secondary and specialist schools. CUSU had liaison support from the Local Education Authority (LEA) to source placements as classroom assistants and provide links to headteach-ers for monitoring and control. The increasing independence of schools from LEA control required increased resources and personnel to have direct contact with schools to source placements. (DBS checks were a given requirement.) CUSU had several motives for initiating the student volunteering programme: to improve relations between students and the local community in a city suf-fering from the negative social aspects of 'studentification'; create socialisa-tion opportunities for the student volunteers (a high percentage reported this as a personal but not exclusive motive); undertake a form of work experience in a sector/field that they wished to explore (a higher priority for the volunteer teaching assistants); to simply 'do good' or give something to the community; to understand the locale and the people (a strong motive for international students); and to build the capacity in the city to receive volunteers (the *sine qua non* strategic issue in all volunteering programmes).

The total number of students grew over the years of MV (1999–2003) onwards. With the formalised system of undergraduates enrolling on modules, the num-ber was limited to between 400 and 500, but with new schemes coming on stream, the number of students at all levels in all types of placements rose close to 1000; students also volunteered outside the module option. Approxi-mately 35% of the 99 schools in the city provided placements.

The student volunteering as classroom assistants had surprising, unintended consequences for all parties: the students, school pupils, teachers and CUSU. In some cases, there were moving narratives of the profound impact the students had in volunteering, which caused deep reflection on their per-sonal motivations and their ability to have an impact. These consequences were not always captured in the formal assessment, but their commitment was celebrated by the university.

The three examples below include one primary, one secondary and one specialist school. They raised questions of gender, aspirations to access Higher Education and changing the National Curriculum respectively.

The primary school

A male geography student was placed in an inner-city primary school with a catchment of low- or no-income, single-parent families. The school had no male staff and most children had no male parent or carer at home. The student's motivation was to consider being a primary school teacher. The impact was twofold, as reported by the headteacher. The children had a male role model for the first time, and he was greeted with enthusiasm by the boys that at last they could pursue male-dominated sports denied to them before. However, all the children benefited from a male figure of responsibility, even if for one term only.

The secondary school

A female modern languages student went on placement at the nearest school to the campus; an inner-city school with a highly diverse catchment area, with over 60 languages being spoken in the area. The student placement was to support French and Spanish teaching. Inevitably, the 13–14-year-old girls became curious about the student's social life, makeup and what it was like being a 'stuck up' student (a bowdlerised version!). The pupils had been disabused of the strange notions of being a student (e.g. they believed students lived in nunnery-like dormitories). Some of the pupils came to see the student as a mentor and, over a term, began to see higher education as a faint possibility for them.

The specialist school

A part-time male student who was recovering from a long and serious illness was placed in a school for the profoundly physically and cognitively disabled. The student had been a full-time undergraduate but the nature of his illness only allowed part-time study and he began judo to enable his physical recovery. On placement, he began to demonstrate basic judo movements and balance and guided the extremely disabled students through some simple moves and throws. The teachers noticed a remarkable improvement in the school students' kinetic and cognitive skills following the demonstrations and lessons. A report by the school principal to the Department for Education and a subsequent investigation resulted in recommendations to all such specialist schools that they adopt programmes involving some form of physical activity (such as judo) to improve cognitive and kinetic skills.

Summary

None of the outcomes of the three cases outlined could have been foreseen: a male role model, a mentor for widening participation in a low participation and highly deprived school, and a change in the National Curriculum for profoundly disabled children. None of the students who volunteered expected to be perceived in these ways. Their motives were prosaic: teaching experience, an interest in inner-city life, an invalid building up his own strength and confidence. There were direct causal consequences in each of these cases: the chance for all pupils to play football, the realisation that university students wore makeup and were not entirely other than them, and a means to improve the skills of disabled students. And none of the receiving schools expected these outcomes when they accepted the placements. The indirect consequences for all parties (the students, the schools, the children) are speculative but of great interest here.

The students found on reflection that their participation in the scheme provided clarity about their roles in society (and careers) and that they could make a difference beyond the formal requirements of the assessment of their placements. Such reflections on social responsibility and impact are rarely included, if at all, in the normal assessments of courses and modules. The respective schools realised that the volunteer placements raised unexpected questions of their own practices: gender balance of staff for child development, widening participation was a deep cognitive problem, and that the curriculum required change. The children will have had varied learning outcomes but for some there would have been profound implications: a male figure who could be trusted by and simply present in the lives of 5–10-year-olds; that it is possible for someone like them to go to university and think of having a career; that some children could be shown that they can move their bodies in ways they never believed they could.

A final pedagogic conclusion: all the parties involved in these and similar volunteering experiences developed a shared narrative about motives, practice and consequences at several levels of causality. This discourse was of an ethical nature of doing good, providing social benefit, being generous, helping others and of self-development in the development of others. None of these aspects of the discourse would be captured in the formal assessment for the curriculum. There was no schema of including the ethical aspects of the practices, which were, it is acknowledged, speculative or required a specific set of assumptions regarding possible outcomes, in the assessment of the students. The disconnection between the lived learning experiences of the students on placement and the actual assessment process was and remains a challenge.

Phil's reflections on student volunteering show the benefits such schemes can have, not only in giving students an authentic experience of 'the real world', but also in easing some of the 'town vs. gown' tensions. Another interesting aspect is the transformational impact that is evident on each of the three students taking part. Finally, it is also striking how the students were able to raise the aspirations of the school students they had been working with.

Another aspect of students engaging with the outside world is through the long-standing history of student activism, usually conducted through the National Union of Students (NUS). For the current generation of students, a key concern is sustainability. The NUS has run an annual survey of student attitudes to sustainability since 2012. The data from the 2018–19 survey (NUS 2019a) shows that an overwhelming majority (80%+) of Higher and Further Education students think that their university or college should be actively promoting sustainable development. Also, 75% of the Further Education respondents thought that sustainable development should be incorporated in their courses. Another interesting result is that 75% of the Higher Education respondents said that they would be happy to sacrifice £1000 in salary to work for a company with a strong environmental and social record.

The last point from the NUS survey is interesting and perhaps reflects the prevailing view that the source of many sustainability problems can be laid at the door of businesses driven by the dominant neo-classical capitalist orthodoxy. To counteract this, many of the world's Business Schools, including most within the UK, are signatories to the UN-sponsored Principles for Responsible Management (PRME). PRME signatories are required to make biannual commitments on how they will promote ethical and responsible business practice. Although a commitment to PRME is essentially faculty-driven, many of the resulting actions, not surprisingly, are focused on students, including many which relate to community engagement. A rich source of examples of the sorts of actions taken by Business Schools in response to their commitments, many of which will be of interest beyond Business School practitioners, can be found in a series of 'Inspirational Guides' published by PRME (PRME 2012, 2013; Murray et al. 2015). In a similar vein, another good source of case studies of students engaging in community-based sustainability activities are the annual Green Gown Awards run by the Environmental Association for Universities and Colleges (EAUC 2020). In 2018, the UN developed the approach taken by the successful PRME initiative and applied it to a broader institutional base through its initiation of the Sustainable Development Goals (SDG) Accord (UN 2020), whereby institutions are invited, in a similar way to PRME, to commit themselves to supporting the delivery of the UN's SDGs in a biannual reporting process.

The second case study in this chapter looks at the response made by the NUS to the findings of their survey outlined above. The approach taken was the development of an accreditation framework called Responsible Futures, which seeks to support the enhancement of Education for Sustainable Development (ESD) through supported, direct institutional change.

Case study 6.2: Responsible Futures – accreditation supporting curriculum change

Paul Cashian, Coventry University

The Responsible Futures (RF) project is an accreditation mark overseen by the NUS aimed at embedding issues around sustainability within the curriculum. The RF accreditation was originally developed partly in response to annual NUS/HEA surveys, which consistently show more than 70% of UK Higher and Further Education students want issues around sustainability to be included within their courses. The RF criteria were developed in association with a range of sustainability-related groups and organisations and was launched in 2014. Eight universities and five Further Education colleges formed the pilot group with the first accreditations being awarded in 2015. Since then the scheme has grown and there are now around 30 universities and colleges that have either gained or are working towards accreditation. More recently, the RF project has been embedded in the wider-ranging Students Organising for Sustainability (SOS) charity established by the NUS.

The stated aim of the RF project is to (NUS 2019b):

"... embed social responsibility and sustainability into teaching and learning. It seeks to legitimise and mainstream education for sustainable development, ultimately helping to ensure students leave education with the knowledge, skills, and attributes needed to lead society to a more just and sustainable future"

One of the cornerstones of the RF accreditation is that it is a partnership between the institution and its Student Union. The underlying principle is that RF should be regarded as a supported change programme. The RF process is meant to provide each institution and its Student Union with a focus for developing a framework to support the enhancement of sustainability education across the institution. The RF project is seen as an on-going process with a biannual review to check progress. Achieving the accreditation mark is not an end in itself but an indication that the institution, in partnership with its students, has put in place an enabling framework to take the whole ESD agenda forward. The involvement of an institution's senior leadership was seen as important given both the focus on developing the curriculum, and the need to move the institutional sustainability focus away from the traditional view that this was an issue for the Estates Department.

What is the accreditation process?

The accreditation process is evidence-based and revolves around putting together a workbook that meets a series of criteria – some criteria are mandatory and some optional plus you can define your own additional criteria if you wish. The mandatory criteria cover areas such as having a RF coordinating partnership group (involving members from the union and the institution) with a clear action plan and evidence of relevant formal and informal curriculum activities. As mentioned previously, the partnership needs a high-level institutional champion who supports the mandatory requirement that an institution's Learning and Teaching strategy supports the objectives of the RF initiative. To achieve the accreditation mark, the workbook evidence is audited by an institution's own students. The audit takes place over a two-day period, with the first day involving the training of the student auditors by NUS staff and a review of the submission. On day two, the student auditors verify the workbook claims by interviewing a range of staff and students before making their final judgement. The accreditation mark is awarded for a period of three years if a minimum score is gained.

What are the benefits and impact of RF accreditation?

Institutions which have been through the RF process identify a range of benefits beyond the obvious potential impact on the curriculum:

- The RF process presents a focal point to draw together a whole range of sustainability-related activities, not just in relation to the curriculum but in extra-curricular and community activities. My experience as part of the initial Coventry coordinating group was that, as we started to gather evidence for our claims against the criteria, we were surprised by just how much evidence there was! We were unearthing a whole range of sustainability activities which had previously been hidden away.
- One strength of the RF process is the requirement for there to be a partnership between the institution and its Student Union. This can act as an opportunity to break down silos between different parts of an institution, forcing debate around sustainability and green issues between parts of an institution that rarely come into contact, e.g. the Student Union and the Estates Department. One thing I learnt from my involvement at Coventry was how perspectives on sustainability and green issues can vary depending on your role and background.
- As part of the RF process, there is a need to undertake a curriculum audit/ review to identify where sustainability and green issues are being addressed. This process can also act as a focal point for wider curriculum issues, and has the added benefit of needing to involve students directly in those discussions.

To conclude, the RF process and accreditation is seen very much as a means to support change by the removal of barriers to the embedding of sustainable education within an institution. The criteria are not prescriptive but are designed to initiate discussion and support the development of ESD. Neither is the process meant to be a 'one size fits all', with three of the 45 criteria being self-defined to capture the distinctiveness of a particular institution's approach.

The case studies in this chapter have highlighted the benefits to students of engaging in the world outside their university or college campus, whether their local communities or the wider societal issues of the day. The emphasis in both was on the impact on the curriculum but both cases illustrate the unintended consequences that are likely to flow from any external engagement, unintended consequences we should expect and embrace.

The NUS's Responsible Futures project, and indeed the PRME initiative in Business Schools, also serve to remind us that the students we are educating today will be the mangers and leaders of the future. The range of ESD initiatives, found in various guises throughout education, need to be about more than just raising awareness of sustainability. As RF and PRME seek to do, they need to influence students in seeking ethical and responsible attitudes and practices which they will carry into their future workplace.

Key takeaways

Universities and colleges play a central role within their local communities, so the more we can engage students within those communities the less the potential for 'town vs. gown' tensions to arise.

As educators, we should be making use of local communities as sources of rich educational experiences for our students. Engaging with the local community either through community-based projects or volunteering schemes can not only be mutually beneficial but can also have enriching, unanticipated consequences, as clearly shown in Case Study 6.1.

Inspired by this chapter? Why not try ...

- *seeking out your sustainability office/team and have a conversation about their strategies and priorities – can they be used as learning opportunities in the classroom?*
- *mapping your modules/course against the UN's SDGs*

7 Widening participation: Access, success and progression

TEF Principles this chapter refers to:

Learning environment: resources and activities to support learning and improve retention, progression and attainment

Student outcomes and learning gain: the extent to which all students achieve their educational and professional goals, in particular those from disadvantaged backgrounds

"Meritocracy (n): a social system, society, or organisation in which people get success or power because of their abilities, not because of their money or social position"

When Tony Blair assumed office in 1997, he declared Britain to be a meritocracy. In a true meritocracy, those who are most talented will rise and therefore society would be structured according to 'merit', so whilst society would remain unequal, it would be due to differences in ability over any other factor (de Main 2017). However, to have a genuine meritocracy, everyone would need to start from the same point – there would be no inherited wealth or private education. We know this is not the case in Britain or across the world. The State of the Nation Report by the Social Mobility Commission (SMC 2019) warned that 'Inequality is still deeply entrenched in Britain … Being born privileged in Britain means that you are likely to remain privileged. Being born disadvantaged however, means that you may have to overcome a series of barriers to ensure that your children are not stuck in the same trap'. The commission believes that social progress can be made by addressing several factors, including high-quality education, which focus on closing attainment gaps. The image presented in Figure 1 illustrates the difference between equality and equity: treating everyone the same versus treating all fairly. Equality can only work if everyone starts from the same place. Equity gives people access to the same opportunities, removing the barriers to participation.

Figure 1 Equality versus equity (*illustration by Adam Chatwin*)

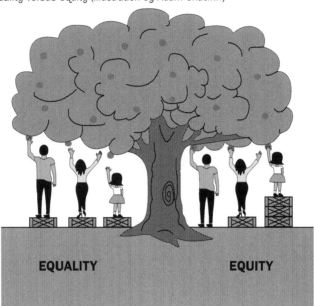

We are led to believe that education is a right not a privilege. Primary and secondary education in the UK is compulsory, but not across the globe. Education is not accessible to all. Thousands of children in Britain are unable to access education due to disabilities, special educational needs or unstable domestic circumstances. The UNICEF report (2018), *An Unfair Start*, focuses on inequality of education in the world's top 41 richest countries, and the results are concerning. The report highlights that some children do worse at school due to circumstances beyond their control; these unfortunate circumstances do not relate to a child's ability. They enter the education system at a disadvantage and education policies often continue to widen the gap between them and their peers. 'Not all children have an equal opportunity to reach their full potential, to pursue their interests and to develop their talents and skills' (2018: 5). Given the data, the ongoing debates around the myths of meritocracy appear to hold true.

In 1997, the publication of *Learning Works* (also known as the 'Kennedy Report') launched the widening participation agenda in Further Education. Within a few years it reached Higher Education, resulting in several government-led policy initiatives directed at addressing under-representation in post-16 education. In 2019, the Office for Students (OfS) implemented a ruling that all Higher Education providers who wished to charge fees above the basic amount must have in force an access and participation plan. The plan has to be approved by the OfS and providers should 'take all reasonable steps to comply with the provisions of the plan' (OfS 2019d). Access and participation plans aim to address equality of opportunity for under-represented groups to '*access, succeed* in and *progress* from Higher Education' (OfS 2019a). There are five key characteristics identified by the OfS which access and participation plans should address:

1 Students from areas of low participation in Higher Education, low household income and/or low socio-economic status
2 Students of particular ethnicities
3 Mature students
4 Disabled students
5 Care leavers

Additional characteristics should also be considered (carers, estranged families, students from Gypsy, Roma and Traveller communities, refugees, learning and/or mental health problems and children from military families). It is not possible to address all of the under-represented groups in this chapter; each deserve far lengthier exploration than is feasible here. Attempts to develop initiatives focused on the individual characteristics listed above can prove to be problematic, and should be handled with care, given an individual may belong to more than one under-represented group. For example, a care leaver may also be a mature student from a low participation area. All providers' access and participation plans are publicly available on their websites. The individual plans provide further information on actions and initiatives regarding access, success and progression.

Access – Getting in

A key aim is to increase the numbers of students from under-represented groups who can access Higher Education, particularly students from socio-economically disadvantaged backgrounds. The Higher Education Funding Council for England (HEFCE) developed the Participation of Local Areas (POLAR) classification, which groups geographic areas into five quintiles (Qn), ranking from Q1 (areas with the lowest participation rates) to Q5 (highest participation rates). Despite ongoing efforts to widen access and participation over the last 20 years, recent figures from the Department for Education suggest that pupils in the most advantaged quintile are more than twice as likely to progress to Higher Education as those from the most disadvantaged quintile (57.9% vs. 26.4%; DfE 2019). Our first case study provides an example of a collaborative initiative which aims to support disadvantaged students transitioning to Higher Education.

Case study 7.1: Further Education to Higher Education – you CAN do it!

Linsey Plant, King Edward VI College, Nuneaton

Nuneaton and Bedworth Borough, Warwickshire has been identified as an area of high deprivation (ONS 2019), with many of the surrounding areas classified as POLAR Q1, the lowest of participation rates. One significant problem has been poor educational attainment at level four, which has ultimately led to low levels of participation in Higher Education (OfS 2018). King Edward VI is a sixth-form college located in Nuneaton, with around 1100 students who attend from the town and surrounding areas. In 2019, the college joined the Better Futures Multi-Academy Trust, which is sponsored by Coventry University.

In 2017, the college embarked on a successful collaboration with Coventry University, the aim being to support students in transitioning from a HNC in Business at the college to a BA Business Management degree at Coventry. The HNC Business is a level four qualification suitable for students who have completed A Levels (or equivalent) and who wish to develop a broad understanding of the business world. Our research suggested that students chose the HNC as they did not feel 'university-ready'; there appeared to be various reasons for this. Some students did not achieve the results they had expected in prior study, which had an impact on their self-efficacy beliefs and levels of confidence. Several of the students did not have peers or family members who had attended university. There exists a wealth of research on students 'first in family' to attend university (see O'Shea *et al*. 2017; Bell and Santamaria 2018) with many linking the lack of family experience to increasing anxieties around expectations of university life. Coventry University is located approximately ten miles from the college, public transport between the two sites being frequent and accessible. This is important, as students from the lowest POLAR4 quintile (Q1) are more likely to study closer to home for a number of reasons. Staying home provides a sense of safety, familiarity and reassurance, students may need to work for financial security and, in some cases, they have caring responsibilities for family members (Reay *et al*. 2010). Students from more disadvantaged backgrounds are more likely to become commuters whilst at university, an emerging area in widening participation discourse (see Thomas and Jones 2017; Maguire and Morris 2018) due to the additional barriers commuting adds to the student experience.

The college and university collaboration began by mapping the HNC to the BA Business Management degree at Coventry. This provided the opportunity for students to jump to level five on joining the programme, removing the need to repeat level four study. The criteria for progression was a pass mark, the same as for students moving from level four to five at university. We recognised the importance of overcoming the barriers to accessing university if students were to be encouraged to progress to Higher Education. The HNC was delivered over one academic year during which a number of initiatives were developed.

Months 0–3: University academics visited students at the college and introduced the university as the next step in their education. Several workshops were jointly led by college and university staff which focused on developing the academic skills required for Higher Education (accessing resources, critical thinking, independent study, academic referencing, etc.). This was supported by weekly personal tutor sessions led by college staff and continuous formative feedback on student assessments.

Months 4–6: Students visited the university for orientation. Their visit featured a number of experiences to include lecture and seminar activities, meeting current students, a campus tour and academic staff Q&A. During this period, academic staff from the university continued to visit the college to deliver guest lectures, provide support and build relationships with the students.

Months 7-9: Students were encouraged to attend university open days and taster sessions. Continued support was provided to students by both college and university staff to familiarise them with the application process and move to university the following academic year. A university mentor was provided to students to support with the transition to level five, and was available for as long as the students required.

The 2017/2018 cohort was a resounding success, with 83% of the students advancing to level five study at university. These students are currently out-performing many of their peers who took the 'traditional' route to Higher Education. One student is currently on a work placement year with Enterprise Rent-A-Car. The results of the collaboration are pleasing for several reasons. All of the students who transitioned to university were the first in their families, some had additional characteristics identified by the OfS, and most had initially planned to end their education once they had completed the HNC. Some of the students have volunteered to return to the college to speak to the current HNC students about their experiences at university. The partnership between the college and university will continue to explore further opportunities to replicate the initiative across additional subject areas.

Recent analysis of university access and participation plans by the OfS suggest that there is a perceived need for greater collaboration (OfS 2020). Linsey's case study provides a good example of this. In 2017, the OfS launched the National Collaborative Outreach Programme (NCOP), which has since been superseded by another programme, Uni Connect. The key aims remain the same, to reduce the gap in participation between the most and least represented groups. Whilst such programmes do have some impact, there is still a long way to go if our aim is to provide Higher Educational opportunities for all students.

For some years, universities and colleges have used contextualised admissions to form a more complete picture of the applicant. Contextual data and information can be used to assess an applicant's prior attainment and potential, in the context of their individual circumstances (UCAS 2017). Contextual admissions may consider an applicant's educational and socio-economic background, their personal circumstances and participation in outreach activities. Our earlier discussion on equality versus equity is relevant here, as some students may require additional support to remove the barriers to participation. However, care must be taken with such measures, as Else (2017) identified in her article, highlighting that differences in students' prior experiences could have the opposite effect of alienation, distancing them further from their peers.

Success – Getting on

Once students arrive at college or university, the next hurdle is to help them to progress and succeed. A key aim of the widening participation agenda is to improve the non-continuation rates of students from under-represented groups, particularly those with disabilities and from minority ethnic backgrounds. On the release of the non-continuation statistics, Chris Millward, Director for Fair Access and Participation at the OfS, stated: 'We know that students from disadvantaged backgrounds are less likely to complete their studies than their more advantaged peers' (OfS 2019b). As academics, we must reflect upon the support we provide for our students to reduce the drop-out rate and encourage our students to succeed. There are a number of factors which have an impact on continuation rates, some of which are embedded in wider societal inequalities and others at a micro level within educational institutions. At the micro level, we have the remit to change our approaches through more inclusive teaching, learning and assessment practices based on student feedback and localised metrics. Personal tutoring has long been the focus of academic and pastoral support for students. The Raising Awareness, Raising Aspirations research project (RARA 2020), led by Sheffield University, uses personal tutoring to increase a student's sense of belonging and access to support. This research highlighted the importance of academic role models, people who can support them in their educational experience. It can help for students to see academics from similar backgrounds to themselves; for example, Binns (2019) suggests that students from more disadvantaged backgrounds are more likely to approach and relate to working-class academics for support and guidance, as they are seen to be more likely to empathise and understand the issues the students are experiencing. This view may well be shared across other widening participation characteristics.

Around 12% of students who are care leavers enter into Higher Education, which is less than among many other disadvantaged groups. Once arriving at university, there are several factors which can impact on their success. Ellis and Johnston (2019) conducted research with care leavers to establish the measures universities can take to better support such students, and made a number of key recommendations. For example, students may arrive without the basic equipment needed, so domestic packages could be provided to include bed linen and a food preparation kit. In addition, it may be more reassuring and comfortable for students to arrive early to better orientate themselves with university life. Care leavers require accommodation that is available 365 days per year; this is vital given there is often no home to return to during study breaks. Appropriate accommodation should also be considered. Several students involved in the research suggested alcohol-free halls, as previous trauma in early years related to alcohol abuse. Throughout their studies, students from a care background should have ready access to support from staff at the university who are trained to provide help as required. Universities across the UK are beginning to offer financial support with tuition fees, accommodation costs and funded field trips.

Gaps in student attainment have been a key focus for a number of years, yet the differences in achievement of students from under-represented groups, particularly from minority ethnic groups and those with disabilities, continue to be of concern when compared to other student groups. In our second case study, Liz, Karen and Dawn explore some of the strategies used at Greenwich to address the gap.

Case study 7.2: Strategies to reduce the black, Asian and minority ethnic (BAME) attainment gap in Business Education

Liz Warren, Karen Brickman and Dawn Reilly, University of Greenwich

Universities in the UK have been working on strategies to widen participation, designed to actively provide opportunities for students from non-traditional backgrounds. While this strategy is delivering a more diverse student population, not all students achieve similar outcomes, despite studying for comparable qualifications (Warren and Reilly 2019). Universities UK (UUK 2019b) argues that for BAME students, the attainment gap can be as great as 13% when viewing students awarded good degrees (first class or upper second class degree classifications). Attainment gaps can arise for multiple reasons; however, as evidenced by UUK (2019b), major concerns are associated with the attainment gap when it applies to groups of students who display different characteristics (HEFCE 2018), for example, demographically, and types of entry qualifications.

This case study focuses mainly on the BAME attainment gap, in a post-92 Business School, which has a student body comprising approximately 6000 students on campus and a further 3000 off-campus. The experience shared will feature a national project, part funded by HEFCE/OfS and led by Kingston University. The University of Greenwich has contributed to the project by implementing strategies to reduce/close the gap. At the University of Greenwich, approximately 50% of students identify as BAME.

The attainment gap strategy used at the Business School, within the University of Greenwich, has focused on the good practice set out by Kingston University. We have implemented and added to their original project (McDuff *et al.* 2018). For example, we measure the attainment gap using a value-added metric, developed by Kingston. This metric is calculated using students' entry qualifications and the specific subjects studied (the two commonly cited factors related to under-achievement), to generate sector-wide benchmarks for the proportion of students expected to achieve a good degree outcome. This benchmark is then compared to the proportion of students awarded a first or upper second classification. Any positive difference between our metric and the sector benchmark signifies value-added. These metrics are used at both the programme level and the module level, and we have created dashboards to enable everyone to access the information.

The first step when addressing the BAME attainment gap is to create a community of practice wherein a conversation is encouraged regarding the issues. Within the Business School, we allocated a work allowance, making it possible for each department to have a lead person to focus on the project. This lead is expected to engage with the University project, and also with other universities, and the dashboards allow each department to identify high-risk areas in order to focus on those. To prevent relevant conversations only happening with a select group of academics, we celebrated projects undertaken by each department by providing a dedicated session in the School's Learning and Teaching

Festival. The Festival provided a platform for each department to share their experiences of addressing the attainment gap with other disciplines.

Some examples of general projects introduced in the first year include:

- Changing teaching materials, such as case studies, to ensure they represent the demographics of our students
- Adapting our language to ensure communications and assessments are inclusive and accessible
- Working with student curriculum consultants to consider the theories and articles used within module designs, with the purpose of reflecting the world more broadly, rather than just taking a Western approach
- Implementing the use of a system so that lectures can be recorded to support students with caring responsibilities, disabilities and second language challenges
- Offering additional courses to support students from non-traditional backgrounds to build social capital
- Creating research projects to enquire why some students with common demographics do not engage in extra-curricular activities

There are also projects underway, to address specific issues identified by individual departments.

The under-representation of BAME industry professionals in the events, hospitality and tourism sectors has been identified as a problem, particularly in relation to female Muslim students. Feedback from students highlighted that their motivation is affected by what they witness in the industry. Therefore, we apply a targeted approach to bringing in a more diverse pool of industry speakers, with whom our students can identify.

In Economics, we worked on social learning, by extending the use of a Team-Based Learning approach in core courses. Our pilot project achieved a reduction in the performance gap between white and BAME students.

In the Accounting and Finance, and Strategy departments, which both have a significant proportion of direct-entry students from China, we undertook a transformational project to provide extra support. Some examples of the measures introduced include offering additional support sessions, changing the way in which we communicate with students and designing non-credit-based modules in order to support the required academic skills not provided on their previous programmes (Reilly *et al.* 2019).

Addressing the attainment gap for BAME students has not been resolved but we are reducing the gaps in some areas already. Our next step is to continue with this project but also to widen it to include other characteristics that are covered elsewhere under the Equality Act. However, it has been encouraging to start to engage in conversations and develop other projects, as ways to address something that has been ignored for too long. It is not yet possible to provide conclusive evidence that the attainment gap has been reduced across the School, because it is too early. To deliver sufficient evidence, we need to refine our dashboards and metrics, so we can focus on individual variables that would contribute usefully to the issues being addressed. Changes take time to implement, and the experience of each student is three to four years. However, what can be reported is that academics are now openly discussing the BAME attainment gap and devising initiatives to reduce it.

The BAME attainment gap has been the centre of analysis for at least the last decade; more recently, discourse has shifted to discussions of an *award* gap. This change in rhetoric stems from a rejection of the deficit model, making institutions responsible rather than the students themselves. Interventions must shift from initiatives which focus on making BAME students work harder; as Akinbosede (2019) states, 'since we know that BAME students are not the problem, why are we asking them to do most of the work in solving it?'

Progression – Moving up

A key question for those accessing and completing their studies is, 'what's next?' For students progressing from Further Education there are a number of barriers, some of which have been discussed earlier in this chapter. The UCAS report *Through the Lens of Students* (2016) explored students' perceptions of university, its key conclusions highlighting the difference between student groups. Students from disadvantage backgrounds (Q1) were most concerned about the cost of accommodation and that other students would be wealthier than them, whereas the more advantaged students (Q5) were worried about establishing a network of friends and fitting in. Higher tariff universities tend to be favoured by more advantaged students, The Brilliant Club (2020) aims to address this by encouraging pupils from under-represented backgrounds to progress to highly selective universities, one of several similar initiatives.

Graduating from university is a joyous time, certainly a celebration for students, families and friends. It is recognition of the hard work, effort and achievement over the previous few years. However, it can also be a very anxious time, as many students try to determine the next step in their life. For some this may be further study, for others it will be entering the workforce. Further and Higher Education providers across the globe invest significant resources in guiding students to successful outcomes. Employability, skills development and initiatives to promote postgraduate studies are a key focus, particularly during the final period of study. It is relatively undisputed that graduates go on to earn more than non-graduates. In some under-represented groups, there is a clear advantage of gaining a degree; for example, the employment rate for students with a disability stands at 72% compared with 46% for those who finalised their studies at GCSE level (Powell 2020). However, there are still some significant differences in the earnings of graduates from students in marginalised groups. Graduates from more deprived backgrounds are less likely to progress into highly skilled employment. Five years after leaving university, students from Q1 earned on average 19% less than those from Q5 (HESA 2017). There are efforts across the sector to reduce these gaps; many provider access and participation plans focus on this area following actions and recommendations specified by the OfS.

Key takeaways

Education plays a pivotal role is providing social mobility opportunities in society. Global inequalities impact on access to, success in and progression from education. To give everyone a chance, equitable approaches are required, which means removing barriers to access in order to allow students to reach their full potential.

We must treat each student as an individual, and this helps us to be inclusive of the minority. Support needs to be tailored to individual needs; one size does not fit all due to the complexity of individual circumstances. The importance of the student voice is paramount to ensure that assumptions are not made regarding possible initiatives and solutions.

Inspired by the chapter? Why not try ...

- *developing and exploring relationships between local colleges and universities*
- *exploring how contextualised admissions are used in your institution – but take care in highlighting differences between students*
- *investigating what support and mentoring is provided for students – is this tailored to individual needs?*
- *reviewing access and participation plans from other Higher Education providers – help to share best practice and initiate collaborative approaches to widening participation across the sector*

8 Internationalisation: The global classroom

TEF Principles this chapter refers to:

Learning environment: resources and activities to support learning and improve retention, progression and attainment

The UK population is becoming more diverse but nowhere is this seen more than in the Higher Education sector. Across the globe, students now have more opportunities to travel for study than ever before, with the numbers in the UK seeing a steady increase. The most recent OECD data indicates that 458,490 international students are studying in the UK, making up almost 20% of the student population; this is matched by 20% international academics teaching in the UK (OECD 2019). Whilst growth in the UK has remained moderate (0.3%), the introduction of two-year post-study visas from 2020 may lead to higher growth in international student applications. The numbers of international students choosing Australia, Canada, the US and Germany have grown by 13.9%, 10.4%, 7.1% and 6.9% respectively (UUK 2019a), demonstrating that greater numbers of students are opting to study away from their home country. These figures have been included here to illustrate a snapshot of diversity in our education settings; we may all experience very different demographics and this will depend upon region, level of study and variances in subject areas. Over the last decade, there have been numerous substantial studies on the growth and priorities of internationalisation (for more, see Knight 2013; Law and Hoey 2018; Wihlborg and Robson 2018); given their scope, any attempts to comprehensively address these here would be futile. We must also be mindful of the volatility of the international student market and various student mobility initiatives. Recent events such as Brexit and the COVID-19 pandemic demonstrate how quickly priorities change, forcing students, academics and the education system as a whole to adapt rapidly to a changing environment.

In this chapter, we turn our attention to what we can do in classrooms to enhance our students' experience in order to ensure they can appreciate the global context in which Further and Higher Education operates. Providing a global learning experience which is equitable and of high quality prepares graduates to contribute to a globally interconnected society. Students and academics should work collaboratively as an international community. The diversity of individuals provides a variety of identities, cultures and experiences that can enrich and enhance learning. Therefore, internationalisation becomes a shared responsibility among organisations, individuals and the curriculum (Advance HE 2019).

Bringing the world to our students: Do they need to 'go away'?

Whilst we may see students from a variety of international backgrounds, around 80% of participants in Higher Education remain home-based students, a figure that is even higher for Further Education. The problem academics have centres on how we can ensure our home students develop a global focus to their education. It is widely regarded that internationalisation is an essential aspect for academic and professional success, with undergraduate students who spend time aboard during their studies having a greater chance of securing a graduate job and of having a higher starting salary than peers who are not mobile. The mobility of home students has been a focus for many universities for some time, yet the numbers remain low. HESA statistics (2018) suggest only 1.6% of UK students travelled abroad for work or study during 2016–17. More recent figures from Universities UK (2019a) include volunteering abroad, so the figure is a little higher at 7.8%. The many examples of opportunities to travel include field trips, study abroad periods, work abroad placement years and volunteering. However, a number of barriers may restrict travel, including finances, health, family commitments and perceived value. In recent years, there have been increasing pressures on organisations and individuals to limit non-essential travel due to concerns around climate change and the environment.

Heffernan *et al.* (2019) have researched the growing interest in internationalisation at home and the importance of developing intercultural awareness for home-based students, with a particular focus on the student's own perceptions and experiences. They found a wide subject-based disparity in the perceived benefits of internationalisation and called for its early adoption at home, initiatives which clearly signpost students towards the importance of enhancing understanding of internationalisation. Interestingly, Heffernan *et al.* found that the reluctance of students to adopt a global approach mirrored staff who were more averse to internationalisation initiatives, suggesting that we as academics need to reflect on our own beliefs and perceptions.

In our first case study, Sathees shares an example of an internationalisation initiative which pairs students from a UK-based university with students from a Higher Education college in Malaysia.

Case study 8.1: Creating opportunities through Collaborative Online International Learning (COIL)

Sathees Kunjuthamby, Coventry University in collaboration with INTI International College, Subang in Malaysia

Identifying different ways of how to scaffold learning remains an important remit for academics, who teach both large (i.e. lectures) and small class sizes (i.e. tutorials, seminars, workshops). With the rise of international student recruitment by many universities, academics are wrestling with how to best introduce a 'blended' teaching approach that connects home/EU students with international students. Whilst many universities claim that they have an internationalisation strategy and that 'internationalisation' is part of everything they do, devotion to the curriculum means there is little engagement. The aim of this case study is to encourage academics to engage with the COIL project as an effective application for internationalisation of the curriculum.

This COIL project requires students from Coventry University and INTI International College to present their internationalisation strategy according to the scenarios provided. With this collaborative opportunity, students are encouraged to become independent learners as well as to work jointly together to demonstrate their creativity, enthusiasm and knowledge in the area of entrepreneurship and international business, and apply the knowledge, models and theories they have been taught in class to a 'practical case'. Following this, both groups of students are expected to deliver a media presentation. This is viewed by their peers as well as by the collaborating partner university with the aim of responding to questions that have emerged from their analysis as well as to engage with peer feedback afterwards. The medium selected for communication as well as for collaborating jointly is the social media platform 'Facebook', for which a closed group with students from both universities was created.

Before starting the COIL project, academics at both institutions explored how they could increase and incentivise student engagement and create materials or a project that would add value to their learning instead of privileging one student group at the expense of the other. In order to motivate early engagement with the assignment, both sets of academics developed a presentation activity with the goal of receiving peer feedback as well as formative feedback from the lecturer. Despite the announcement that the presentation as well as the Q&A session were not part of the assessment, students from Coventry University as well as INTI International College were engaged throughout and there was clear evidence of collaboration to improve each other's work. The COIL project was developed jointly between the two institutions with the sole purpose to work collaboratively on the content, pedagogy and internationalisation of the curriculum. In other words, to exchange ideas and knowledge, to work collaboratively, to receive constructive feedback and benefit from a variety of examples that are relevant for the learning on their modules – proving that collaboration transcends national economies.

The COIL project

Academics from both institutions created a welcome video, which together with photos of the groups were uploaded to the private Facebook page. Students were invited to join an ice breaker activity where they introduced themselves by uploading a short video outlining their background and future aspirations.

The second activity required students to complete a consultant-led activity and create a video presentation; these were shared with other students for peer review and formative feedback. The activity focused on specific international markets, which reinforced peer learning of various social, cultural and ethical environments. Peer review exercises were focused with specific questions asked of each group, for example, prompting recommendations about further strategy and developing a set of enquiries about the activity.

Feedback from both academic staff and students was overwhelmingly positive. Academic colleagues complimented Sathees for his guidance and support in initiating and operationalising the COIL project, one stating: 'I intend to continue working on similar projects in the near future, as I truly believe that through innovation and application, the teaching and learning experience of the lecturers and students can be further enhanced'. In addition, Sathees has led and supported academics in several similar projects where students from Coventry University have worked with students from across the globe, including in Oman, Hong Kong, Spain, Malaysia and France. Student engagement, feedback and appreciation has been positive.

"This was a collaboration between three universities and this project helped us to understand how important it is to work in teams but has also offered us an opportunity to see how students from different countries are taking the same case study questions, for example, in a different direction with a different analysis"

(Undergraduate final year student, Hong Kong COIL project)

"The COIL Project launched by Sathees is a great initiative that allowed me to work with students of different nationalities together with the same objective. Good job!"

(Undergraduate final year student, Spain COIL project)

Recommendations for developing a COIL project

- Familiarise yourself with available digital/communication tools – this will help you to select the applications to use for the COIL activities that you and your collaborator have designed
- Identify a partner who wishes to collaborate on a COIL project
- Identify whether you and your partner are teaching in the same academic semester
- Exchange the syllabus of your modules and identify areas for COIL collaboration
- Draft a COIL proposal and jointly develop it with your partner
- Confirm the activities, COIL outputs to be created and deadlines as well as which digital tools are to be used for the COIL project/communication

- Announce on the first day of your teaching the COIL project alongside the deliverables, duration and date of completion
- Keep in touch with your COIL collaborator on a regular basis to ensure the completion of the COIL project
- Provide your formative feedback in a timely fashion as announced to the students
- Ensure engagement of your students – the same is expected at your partner institution
- Collect feedback for areas of improvement as well as how this provides added value to the students

In this case study, Sathees provides an example of how students can engage in international exposure without leaving the country. Through experiential learning with peers across the globe, students can gain a greater understanding of the differences and similarities experienced in a safe, supported environment. We must also recognise that diversity exists in our classroom. Our cohorts may include students and staff from a number of different countries, but we need also to consider that our home students may have a myriad of prior international experiences. As Fielden states, 'an important part of internationalization at home lies in creating a vibrant international community for learning and research' (2011: 39); we should therefore embed global thinking at the earliest opportunity.

Internationalisation of the curriculum, which has been a key focus in education for some time, requires it to take on global dimensions. An internationalised curriculum, as stated by Leask (2009: 205), 'will engage students with internationally informed research and cultural and linguistic diversity'. Our role as academics is to facilitate the development of our students' international perspectives as global citizens. There are many ways to approach this and the first consideration is to ensure that internationalisation is embedded in the course design, through learning outcomes, programme aims, and the overall teaching and learning philosophy. We should then turn to the curriculum, scholarly materials and activities used within the teaching environment. It might be tempting to use familiar case studies and examples but, if focus is on a single region, it will prevent the development of global awareness. For example, UK-based cases will benefit home students who will be in a stronger position than international students to understand them. Wherever possible, cases that have an international context will support the development of knowledge and cross-cultural awareness of all students in the cohort. Academics may also ask international students to provide examples from their country of origin and compare these amongst one another, which has the added benefit of more active participation and student engagement.

Within some contexts it may be possible to invite guest lecturers and speakers from global industries. We saw from Sathees' example in Case Study 8.1 that location need not be a barrier. Technology can be used to introduce speakers from across the globe, and students can engage live with international experts and discuss or question the impact of various theories and cases without leaving the classroom. In our second case study, Emily explores the issue of raising the confidence of British students to explore global concepts without leaving the classroom.

Case study 8.2: An international outlook in a fixed curriculum

Emily Atkinson, Higham Lane Sixth Form

Students studying A Level Sociology at Higham Lane are predominantly British and live in the local area. As there are few international students or staff, opportunities to access global cultures and lived experiences are limited. Providing the students with an international outlook within a fixed curriculum is a key challenge. Globalisation is included in the Sociology curriculum. This element of the course has been given more emphasis since the introduction of the revised A Level curriculum in 2015. The relevance of globalisation in society today has never been more pertinent; however, when delivered in a UK education setting, which lacks international diversity in the classroom, the challenge to ensure the subject is stimulating and relatable is heightened. As a result, students have struggled to fully understand global perspectives. This case study explores some activities embedded in the class to try and increase the students' confidence and ability to think critically about the global impact of key sociological concepts.

It is important to build confidence and awareness over a period of time, introducing concepts of globalisation in stages to encourage knowledge retention and the ability to critically debate issues.

Step 1: Building awareness

It is often the case that students are not immediately aware of the impact of globalisation on their lives and surrounding environment. It is vital to increase awareness so that students can appreciate both the world outside their local environment and, essentially, the influence and connectedness of globalisation on their lives and community. For the students in this case, we established a series of activities to build awareness, the first being a global bingo game. The students were provided with a sheet containing a number of experiences, items, networks, hobbies and foods, all with an international link. They were tasked with identifying the experiences that they had personally participated in during the previous week. Examples taken from the bingo sheet included acts such as: ordering shopping from overseas, using social media to talk to someone outside the UK, eating a food sourced from another country, supporting an international sports team, listening to an international pop star and wearing fashion products manufactured outside of the UK. This activity was a simple but effective way of allowing students to recognise how each and every one of them was linked to a global and not just a local society on a daily basis, thus raising awareness of globalisation. A visual representation of the findings from the bingo activity was provided via a world map displayed in the classroom. This activity provided a visual artefact to support the development of students in seeing the wider impact of globalisation on their daily lives. A second activity to further deepen their understanding of the global society involved a consideration of the impact of removing these opportunities, activities and networks. Students were encouraged to discuss their findings with their peers.

Step 2: Building confidence

Once students have developed a level of awareness, it is important to increase their confidence in understanding concepts on a larger scale. There are a number of subjects on the Sociology curriculum which require students to have a deeper understanding of globalisation and the international landscape. Some of the topics can be deemed 'tricky' and require careful scaffolding in a safe environment to support students in their open discussions. In this case, the task was framed around sociological perspectives, focusing on postmodernist views. This encouraged students to recognise how life has changed and how some of the issues we encounter now are different to those experienced in less globalised times. The students were given an activity which asked them to explore some of the examples provided in Step 1 and how things have changed over time. For example, how has fashion changed now we can source overseas materials? How have our diets changed now we can import food from other countries? Once students started to demonstrate confidence in these discussions, the activity moved on to trickier subjects such as the global impact on local crime (drug supply chains) and the movement of people (refugees and sex trafficking). Working in small groups, students were asked to take a local matter, explore the international impact, then present this back to the rest of the class. It was imperative to ensure that there were clear ground rules to the activity, particularly given such topics can lead to emotive discussions on matters such as gender roles, ethnicity, stereotypes and religion.

Step 3: Consolidating understanding

As awareness was raised and confidence established, students began to have more meaningful and informed discussions on topics in the curriculum. These included:

- Gender roles and culture
- Immigration and changing family structures
- Globalised health industry
- Impact of globalisation on work and poverty
- Global education policy

Given the assessment is linear and all knowledge is assessed at the end of a two-year period, it is essential that students develop an in-depth understanding of the global impact on sociological concepts in Britain. Activities throughout the course are led by students who are encouraged to independently seek international examples which can then be applied to the fixed curriculum.

There is a tendency to launch straight into the set curriculum; however, as a result of the three-step approach described, students at Higham Lane developed a greater understanding of what it means to live in a 'global village' (McLuhan 1962). Students developed more confidence in discussing global topics, a greater awareness of global issues and the ability to think more holistically about the impact of sociological theory outside of their own cultural experiences.

In Emily's case study, we can see how important it is to reset students' expectations from the outset. Across the world there are similar education settings where students have not had international experiences, and where the classroom lacks diversity in terms of both students and teachers. This dynamic contrasts with what we may experience in many Higher Education settings and challenges our assumptions regarding existing awareness of global perspectives.

Too many potatoes?

The international nature of our student cohorts in Higher Education provides all students with the opportunity to adopt a global outlook, and such international skills are important in a highly diverse world. However, there are some well-documented challenges to internationalisation, particularly when students originate from a wide variety of locations worldwide. These include language barriers, cultural differences, diverse expectations and prior educational experiences. Care must be taken to avoid treating students as a homogeneous group, because in doing so we fail to celebrate the diversity of international students while also encouraging home students to be viewed as a uniform group with similar prior experiences. Scudamore (2013: 3) suggests that, '[i]f we accept that there is diversity within student groups as well as between them, and that there are commonalities between all students, then [internationalisation approaches] can be seen to be of benefit to all students and not just international students'. It is important to create a learning environment where differences are explored and discussed in a transparent and respectful manner – the use of mutually agreed ground rules can support this. During a seminar at the beginning of the first year, we encouraged students to identify and discuss cultural stereotypes. To encourage contributions, we asked international students to share their initial experiences of living in the UK. One student from China stated, 'I do not understand your obsession with potatoes, you eat them nearly every day'. Some students were baffled to begin with, but it led to a valuable discussion where stereotypes were addressed and many myths busted. There are numerous activities which can be used to structure such discussions – take a look at Scudamore's (2013) article for some further ideas. Care must be taken to ensure that discussions remain professional and do not lead to unnecessary upset or student disengagement. For academic staff, it is important to recognise that students are likely to have different and often more global experiences than oneself, so it is essential that a reflective approach is used with the knowledge that you do not need to have all the answers: this is a good opportunity to view students and academics as co-learners. As academics, we need to be reflective and challenge our own assumptions regarding our learners and recognise that we may take for granted understanding regarding academic regulations and policies.

All students enter a new education setting with a variety of different experiences, something that is evident among both home and international students.

Experiences and expectations can be very different, yet Further and Higher Education tends to avoid any differentiation; the methods of teaching and learning remain the same regardless of prior experience. Any form of differentiated learning becomes more challenging when dealing with large cohorts. One approach would be to reset the students' expectations from the outset, bridging the gap between differences in experience and expectation. This could involve activities which introduce all students to Further or Higher Education and support students in educational processes and policies. A number of universities have seen some success with pre-enrolment activities conducted via email, and online support which covers organisational aspects of the programme such as lecture times, assessment types, key contacts and overall topics studied. This could be followed by study skills workshops in the first semester, which might address topics such as referencing techniques, assessment planning, critical thinking, support services and accessing online systems.

As academics, we often find that students tend to align themselves with those who share similar ethnicities. In a culturally diverse classroom, students are sometimes reluctant to integrate with other cultural groups. Guidance often suggests that tutors should manage group composition and instigate cross-cultural group work. Brown (2013) suggested that the active integration of international and home students should be promoted. This requires advance preparation to set up the mixed groups and ongoing encouragement for the students to work together. Whilst this may be a positive approach, it is important to recognise that students purposely choose to mix with similar peers for a number of reasons, including less anxiety around language and a mutual understanding of cultural norms. If groups are to be mixed, it is vital to ensure students are aware of the reasons why: learning gains, greater cultural awareness and peer learning across international perspectives. If assessments are to be group based, then it is recommended that an element of formative evaluation and feedback is included to allow the students to develop their skills prior to final assessment. An alternative to initiating mixed groups might be to permit students to form their own groups, and tasks could focus on them presenting the results of research and discussions to the wider student cohort. Such an approach would still support the sharing of knowledge but without the pressure of forced groupings.

In a discussion with a student during a pastoral meeting, she raised some concerns about making friends at university and that she was finding it quite difficult. Further discussion uncovered that she felt, because she was of Chinese appearance, home students tended to avoid her despite being born in the UK, where she had lived all her life. She also stated that tutors would sometimes ask her to share her experiences from her home country, but that by saying she was British she felt she might be construed as being confrontational. As academics, we must ensure that we are careful in our approaches to internationalisation. There is a tendency to draw upon prior experience or cultural stereotypes, when doing so could be harmful to our students. We must reflect upon our own practices and views to create a positive learning environment for all.

Key takeaways

Students can be encouraged to take up the variety of mobility initiatives available to them; those that do often demonstrate enhanced life skills and make memories that last a lifetime. Travelling across the world might be life affirming but we know this might not be possible for everyone for a variety of reasons. Home students who remain at home can develop global perspectives through meaningful cross-cultural experiences within the classroom. It is vital to embed internationalisation into the curriculum, but to do so requires a strategic focus which weaves internationalisation into the fabric of educational institutions.

In her book, *Becoming*, Michelle Obama reflects on her experience at Princeton University, particularly the approach used by academics to enforce heterogeneous harmony. She states, 'The burden of assimilation is put largely on the shoulders of minority students' (2018: 74). As academics, we need to reflect on our approaches to building awareness of internationalisation and ensure that we do not view students as members of homogeneous groups. Instead, we are co-learners, and the richness of our students' experiences benefit all who are part of the education journey. We must also ensure that we create safe, comfortable learning environments which do not unfairly exploit students' backgrounds and experiences for the benefit of others. Efforts to assimilate students into UK-centric methods of education can create a deficit model, one which adversely affects international students and fails to respect alternative perspectives (Scudamore 2013). Inclusive approaches to internationalisation are essential. Each student, regardless of background or origin, presents a unique perspective from which others can learn.

Inspired by this chapter? Why not try ...

- *conducting a review at programme level to ensure internationalisation is embedded in learning outcomes and programme aims*
- *identifying local voluntary groups with a cultural, ethical or religious focus and promote the involvement of students in activities and causes*
- *developing authentic assessments where students are encouraged to self-source case studies from global organisations and environments*
- *inviting contributions from academics and organisations across the globe, utilising technology to limit the barriers of location*
- *encouraging a culture of internationalisation amongst academics through regular awareness-raising events – for example, world foods sharing, recognising various religious or cultural ceremonies and celebrations*

Part 3

Student Outcomes and Learning Gain

9 Gaming and simulation

> **TEF Principles this chapter refers to:**
>
> *Learning environment: resources and activities to support learning and improve retention, progression and attainment*
>
> *Student outcomes and learning gain: the extent to which all students achieve their educational and professional goals, in particular those from disadvantaged backgrounds*

"Engage (v): to become involved, or have contact, with someone or something"

The traditional lecture remains a staple of university education despite multiple attempts to change things (de Neve and Heppner 1997). The passivity it engenders has been challenged by such initiatives as the flipped classroom (O'Flaherty and Phillips 2015), interaction within smaller seminar groups and also through the use of digital technology such as Kahoot, Top Hat and Socrative. These initiatives are all designed to ensure that students are not merely empty vessels being filled with knowledge; instead, they become active as co-creators of knowledge (Power and Holland 2018). Within Further Education, although lectures are somewhat rarer, the pressure to increase class sizes and the focus on the passing of assessments (Coffield and Williamson 2011) has meant that there is a tendency to treat lessons as a way of passing on knowledge in order to help students with their work, rather than as an interactive process. This has the effect of making learning instrumental in nature with students focused on the end result rather than on engaging in the learning process.

The model followed in Further and Higher Education in the UK tends to focus on a pedagogical view of learning rather than one which holds andragogical principles at its core (Knowles 1984). This suggests that knowledge is something that is held by the lecturer and their job is one of communicating it rather than releasing it from within the student. Andragogy, by contrast, presupposes that learners are autonomous beings who are able to take control of their learning (Knowles 1984). The two approaches are often characterised as the 'sage on the stage or the guide at the side' (King 1993), and whilst there is undoubtedly a place for the former, the latter has proved more problematic to embed within Further and Higher Education. In part, this has been down to students' previous experiences, although it is important not to overlook students' expectations when addressing this topic.

Bates and Kaye (2014) detail the changing demands of students since the advent of increased tuition fees and the resultant shift in how they view their role. Whilst traditionally a lecturing style has been the norm, seminars and workshops have been used extensively to encourage students to engage with the material. However, with the increased cost of education in the UK, expectations have moved away from taking control of learning towards receiving what the Office for Students (OfS) stresses is 'value for money' (2019d). For educational establishments, this can be a tricky concept because as we saw in Chapter 1, a college or university education is likely to be classified as a service rather than a product and whilst buying a product may be viewed as a transactional arrangement and value for money might well be measured in quantitative terms, value for money for a service would be described as 'immersion in an experiential context' (Cova and Dalli 2009: 318). Clearly, the former is more straightforward to measure and so is often used when evaluating education (Woodall *et al.* 2014). However, if we take the co-creators approach as being preferable, then it is the latter that needs to be addressed.

This then leads us to the question of how you engage learners within this environment. If we accept that learning is a two-way process and the lecturer can only do so much, then it is vital that learners become involved in the process of learning. The problems start, however, when we attempt to work out how to do this, whilst simultaneously making sure that they understand the purpose of what they are doing and also that they have the necessary skills and confidence to participate. Our first case study illustrates one way in which this has happened.

Case study 9.1: Bringing pantomime into education

Professor Ian Turner, Centre for Excellence in Learning and Teaching, University of Derby

Active learning approaches that involve learners as participants in their learning experience have been widely demonstrated to have positive impacts on students' academic engagement and attainment (Prince 2004). However, the rise in student numbers and the increasing use of large classrooms/lecture theatres for teaching is often perceived to be 'at odds' with an active learning approach. It is the perception of many that the range of interactive approaches that can be employed in the classroom decreases as the class size increases. This can often result in the facilitator using more didactic approaches.

The solution proposed here was driven by a desire to 'bring to life' the subject matter and allow students to feel like they are an active part of the experience, despite being part of a large class. The inspiration came from pantomime, which has a rich history originating in ancient Greece. A pantomime is a story-driven form of art which has many parallels to a modern lecture theatre. Pantomime uses scenery (represented by PowerPoint in a lecture), lights and simple props to create an atmosphere or mood for the actors. Using simplistic tropes such as 'they are behind you' and emotional responses (cheering/booing), the members of the audience feel as though they are a part of the story. These ideas were adapted into lecture theatre pantomime (LTP) that focuses the experience on visual stimuli (props, actions and actors) to introduce the subject. The lecture theatre (layout, lights) and equipment (sound and PowerPoints) are in the background and are used to create the atmosphere.

An LTP approach has been successfully incorporated into sessions such as an introduction to the immune system. The pantomime narrative is focused around the fictional invasion of a castle (body) by a Viking horde (pathogens) and the roles of the soldiers (phagocytes) and scientists (lymphocytes) in the battle. Each component of the immune system fits into the analogy – for example, dendritic or antigen presenting cells are 'soldiers' looking to capture rather than kill the enemy. The pantomime is delivered with the aid of costumes, hats and props and delivered using a pseudo-analogy (fictional characters and real scientific terms used concurrently). LTP has been used in a range of other scenarios, including the teaching of the DNA central dogma (Turner 2014).

Student feedback on LTP has always been overwhelmingly positive, with students consistently evaluating the experience in the 'most positive' bracket (>90%) in the end-of-module evaluations. LTP has also been shown to have a positive effect on student attainment. For example, using LTP on the central dogma resulted in a mean grade boundary increase in student examination scores. Students often report on how LTP changes their perceptions and engagement of a subject: 'liveliness makes the lecture much more interesting and engaging'; 'makes me want to learn as it is more fun'.

LTP may present a risk in how it is received by students. Experience has shown my level three (Year 0) and level four (Year 1) students are much more receptive to this form of delivery. Though not observed personally, others have reported, whilst active engagement approaches (like LTP) do improve engagement and attainment for most students, for others it can inversely affect their enjoyment (Smith and Cardaciotto 2011). The gamified and fun approach to teaching is sometimes viewed as undermining the 'seriousness' of Higher Education. LTP content and mapping to learning outcomes is probably far more extensive than one that is traditionally delivered.

LTP may initially seem like an enormous challenge to implement and the reality is that it does take some time to fully develop. It is also fair to say it requires an 'uninhibited' exuberant type personality to execute it to full effect. The best way to develop LTP is to focus on small parts of a session rather than the whole thing. Challenge yourself to think of analogies (the heart of LTP) to explain areas of the subject that students traditionally find most challenging. Consider what props could be physically displayed (or passed around the classroom) to help visualise abstract concepts or bring something to life.

Although active learning is a relatively embedded concept in education that seeks to ensure that students participate in experiential learning (Bonwell and Eison 1991), what Ian describes takes this further and might be described as a simulation involving engaging students' interest through their imagination in a subject and then getting them to apply this knowledge. Whilst a traditional lecturing style might well get the same information across successfully, what is being described is an effort not to merely view the lecture in transactional terms but instead to fully engage students in their learning by stimulating their interest in a subject. This is done by removing students from their expected frames of reference and instead making use of cognitive processes designed to think about new situations. The hope would be that not only would students be engaged when in the lesson but that they would both remember the learning and also seek to expand their knowledge after the formal learning in the lesson has ended.

Clearly this approach is likely to take students out of their 'comfort zone' and because of this, it can be met with some resistance. Passivity amongst students, especially in a lecture, is seen by many as an expected state and whilst some students are able to switch from this presupposition to an active learning approach, for most there needs to be a degree of preparation. Lewin (1958) described the processes for managing any change in terms of 'unfreezing' the status quo and this is what is needed when adopting new approaches. Participants need to be aware of what they gain from a change of approach and this means that communication is of vital importance. It is likely that the simulation explained in our first case study has worked best with Year 0 and Year 1 students, as these students have had only limited previous experience in Further or Higher Education and hence there has not been time for habits and expectations to form. With more experienced students, greater preparation would be needed to encourage them away from their traditional approaches.

There are numerous other advantages in taking this approach and these often relate to developing students' wider skills. Whilst not wanting to delve into the debate about the purpose of education, one pertinent argument is that lecturers need to prepare students for the world of work and hence the development of employability skills can be used as a justification for changes in the curriculum (Rich 2015). By introducing simulation into the curriculum, students are given the opportunity to develop social skills which are likely to not have been developed as much beforehand. In addition, they are being asked to take into account new approaches and new ways of working which can have beneficial effects on their flexibility and how they adapt to new situations.

Taking students out of their comfort zone can prove difficult to manage and it is important to be aware of the potential problems that might be faced. Aside from the importance of 'unfreezing' students ready for the change as directed by Lewin (1958), it is also important to recognise that everyone has a number of personas that make up their character and that encouraging them to try something new is likely to mean that they move from one to another. Goffman (1956) used imagery of the theatre, an apt comparison given the subject of our first case study, to explore the concept of persona. Students are likely to have a 'frontstage persona' (Goffman 1956) that they present in a lecture or traditional lesson setting. Whilst students are happy for this persona to be visible in any educational setting, their backstage persona (which might be viewed as their true self), which they normally keep hidden, might well be exposed when using these techniques, which can mean that students feel more vulnerable than they normally would.

Whilst the simulation approach to learning does take students out of their comfort zone there are alternatives that can be used to demonstrate transferrable skills whilst feeling like a safer option. One such option, gamification, is the subject of our second case study.

Case study 9.2: Problem-based learning

Safaa Sindi, Director of the Business Simulation Suite, Coventry University

Current traditional methods of teaching and engagement have pivoted towards the incorporation of innovative learning. As students' environment changes, so have the approaches to education. Common challenges in teaching are found in maintaining student engagement and methods of improving the retention of information. This challenge has recently increased with globalisation, as most classrooms contain international students, who generally have disparate past experiences of education. There have been various learning theories developed over the years that aim to tackle these challenges, however, I found that Piaget's cognitive theory (1952) and problem-based learning (PBL) are key approaches, as they cater for various learning methods such as taking notes, use of visual aids and practical application.

When constructing lessons around Piaget's cognitive theory, it's best to incorporate the 'schema' processes, which are building blocks of knowledge that create mental links for students to understand and respond to situations (Wadsworth 2004). The schema process creates a ladder-like learning where each lecture is designed to build knowledge from the previous one. Combining this process with PBL ensures students from various backgrounds and with various skills retain the core elements of the lecture.

The PBL approach is done using simulation activities that are delivered in seminars, to allow students to work in small groups and increase the one-to-one support offered. Sessions that incorporated the use of simulation games showed the effectiveness of combining both Piaget's cognitive theory and PBL. An example of this is demonstrated with the Beer Distribution Simulation Game, which is played online, where learners can either play individually or in teams. In the game, learners are tasked to distribute beer from a brewery to a retailer, without accumulating a large inventory, while maintaining enough of a stock level to respond to demand (Lee *et al.* 1997). The simulation game gives learners an idea of the obstacles facing distribution of a batch of beer through its supply chain (e.g. surge in demand), as they reflect on how they can mitigate these obstacles. The aim of this PBL activity is to help learners understand the 'Bullwhip Effect' (a common problem in supply chain management) that leads to surges in inventory, caused by problems of miscommunication and unpredicted lead-times. Whilst it is a relatively simple concept, it is tricky for learners to comprehend in a traditional lecture, but far easier if demonstrated practically. The game is played over two rounds, first with incomplete information and then with complete information. The game is designed to give a practical illustration of the Bullwhip Effect and learners are briefed on its application in the Beer Distribution Simulation Game at the start. Learners are given instructions for round one and asked to play, before repeating the experience in round two. Upon the completion of both rounds, learners are asked to reflect on the supply chain theory application, as well as providing some ideas on how the effects can be mitigated. This allows them to demonstrate their understanding on the issues of having high or low inventory levels.

The consensus from the activity with my students was that in order to maintain inventory levels, they needed to improve the information flow between the wholesaler and the manufacturer, indicating that inventory levels are dependent on complete information and transparency. This helped their critical analysis of the problems and to find solutions to real-world scenarios from the simulation game. The activity helped create a positive climate in the classroom, where students could question, reflect and share their ideas (Hamza and Griffith 2006). It also introduced a level of competition, with each team looking to 'win' the task by staying on top of orders. The use of simulation in learning through gamification increased the international students' participation, due to the removal of barriers found in traditional teaching environments, such as problems with communication. Furthermore, the use of gamification helped my students to interact and gain confidence, especially those who were often reluctant to participate. The students gave positive feedback, with the consensus being that they wanted to have more simulation learning and gamification, as it helped them visualise concepts and encourage them to share ideas in a relaxed environment.

This exercise was also used by seminar tutors, who found that using gamification in a PBL teaching method helped students develop their own way of learning, as those who preferred note taking, put themselves forward in their group to be in charge of writing ideas, while those who preferred practical application found ways to help formulate the group ideas into practical solutions.

In this case study, the simulation game is aimed at a specific learning outcome, where students learn issues about the Bullwhip Effect in the supply chain, from the upstream (purchasing of raw materials), midstream (distribution and manufacturing) and downstream (wholesaler and retailer or end consumer). Tutors can select suitable simulation and gamification methods for their specific learning outcome, by following a framework developed by Ertmer and Newby (2013). The task is to first understand how students learn, then how learning occurs, and finally analyse the factors influencing student learning. This will enable them to determine the basic principles that are relevant in assessing and designing a high-quality interactive session using simulation and gamification.

The use of simulation and gamification helps improve student engagement, as shown from the student feedback. As students' environment changes, so should the methods of education. The incorporation of PBL or experiential learning helps students gain a skill-based education that contributes to their employability. This provides an innovative edge to traditional teaching methods, which involve passive learning, while incorporation of simulation and gamification focuses on active learning through practical application. Hence, there is a growing need to adapt and provide a learning and teaching perspective that aims to enhance student engagement and achieve better learning outcomes.

Safaa's case study highlights two key areas in which gamification – which can be defined as the process of introducing elements of games into the learning process (Werbach 2014) – can help. Clearly, the first one is ensuring students are able to take control of their learning and gain new, transferrable skills in a social learning setting. This allows learning to go beyond a transactional relationship with a pedagogical core towards one that is more andragogical in nature that is close to the concept of discovery learning (Bruner 1961). This means that students become active participants in their learning and become engaged in the process rather than take a role as passive bystanders whose only interest is in the outcome. This also means that the transfer of theory to practice becomes much more straightforward for students as they are doing this themselves rather than being the passive learners discussed above.

There are problems with taking this approach and our second case study hints at them. Learners are likely to come from disparate backgrounds and most are unused to taking this approach to their learning. This means that there is often a period of adjustment which can detract from the lesson. In addition to this, it also necessitates the lecturer to relinquish control of the class to a greater degree than in a more traditional lesson. Whilst this can have great benefits in terms of the lesson and also the lecturer's workload, it can cause problems in a sector where there has been a move towards a more homogeneous pattern of delivery. New lecturers gain the inculcated knowledge that there is 'one way of doing things' through a combination of institutional reinforcement, mentoring and quantitative measures of performance and this means that using these techniques can be seen as a risk.

Using simulation and gamification also changes the classroom dynamic and means that the participants change role. In a traditional lecture or lesson, the classroom is a place of delivery; when using simulation or gamification, it takes on a role that is more akin to the theatre described in our first case study. This means that the role of both the lecturer and the students alter as well. To return to Goffman's (1956) dramaturgical approach, our first case study shows, to good effect, that the classroom can change to a setting where students are at the centre of the learning process. In turn, this then alters the role of the lecturer as they have to take on a different frontstage persona (Goffman 1956). Rather than leading the learning, their persona changes to one whereby they are guiding students and making sure that they engage in the learning process. This can be a challenge with students who are either not prepared or unwilling to participate.

As well as improving the linkage between theory and practice, gamification can also be used to introduce an element of competition within the classroom. This can have the benefit of maintaining interest for students who are keen to 'win' and see learning as a side effect of this process. In some subjects (such as Business Studies), it can also have the benefit of teaching students the skills that are linked to the subject so that both the knowledge and the application of that knowledge can be demonstrated.

Key takeaways

The goal of any lecturer is to ensure that students engage with the material being taught and the aim of this chapter is to suggest alternative ways of doing this through both gamification and simulation. These techniques are designed to move students out of their established comfort zones and encourage them to both apply the learning and test it out themselves. These techniques move students away from a pedagogical approach towards one that is andragogical in nature. This means that they take control of their learning far more and the lecturer relinquishes some control of the learning. What this creates is a situation whereby students are able to see the application of the knowledge they are learning and also gain new skills. They will also be using skills that are not always apparent in a traditional lecture such as using their imagination, problem-solving skills and also their competitive instincts. All of these can be beneficial to both their engagement in the lesson and also their interest in the subject after formal teaching has ceased.

These benefits are not gained without a degree of risk. Many students are likely to be unaware or inexperienced in the techniques described and hence careful coaching is needed. The unfreezing of previous frames of reference is a necessary part of the process but can be time-consuming and frustrating for both staff and students, as there is no tangible outcome during these sessions. However, once the preparation has been done, there are numerous benefits:

- This method of teaching can motivate learners, as it gives them the opportunity to learn in a different manner
- There is a benefit to using a more social form of learning, as students can learn from each other and also interact far more than they would using more traditional techniques
- The transference of theory to practice is much easier to achieve when learners can see the practical application of what they are doing
- Competition can be a beneficial learning tool – it can encourage students to try new approaches in the hope that they will beat other students
- By moving students out of their comfort zone, you can give them greater confidence in their own ability and willingness to take risks

It is important to note, however, that there are risks attached to using this method of learning. These include:

- The preparation time can be a problem, as not only do you have to prepare resources but you must also prepare your students for the activity
- Not all students like this approach, as it can take them out of their comfort zone
- Some students will not see this as 'learning' and hence, there may be resistance (especially with more experienced students)
- It does mean that as a lecturer you need to relax your control of your class a little more than normal – there is transference of responsibility for learning to students and this can be difficult to do

A traditional classroom is often described as one where the lecturer is at the front and the students are in a passive state, absorbing what they are told and trying to make sense of it. Gamification and simulation change this around and allow students to participate far more in the process. The role of the lecturer changes from that of the expert imparting knowledge to that of a facilitator who is getting students to understand things for themselves. Whilst this can be daunting for both lecturer and students, the benefits can be significant and result in students engaging in their studies far more than before.

Inspired by this chapter? Why not try ...

- *using role play to get students to empathise with particular points of view*
- *getting students to enter competitions with other providers when using gamification*
- *encouraging students to apply their previous experiences to a seminar problem*
- *using simulation software to apply knowledge*
- *developing a sense of belonging through student-led communities within programme/course boundaries*

10 Authentic assessment

By Colette Ankers de Salis and Christine Smith,
Liverpool John Moores University

TEF Principles this chapter refers to:

Student outcomes and learning gain: the extent to which all students achieve their educational and professional goals, in particular those from disadvantaged backgrounds

Assessment is integral to education – we have to test knowledge and understanding in some way, as this is how we measure attainment across both the Further and Higher Education sectors. However, assessment continues to be a frustration for academic staff and students alike; in fact, satisfaction rates are consistently the lowest for assessment and feedback in the National Student Survey year on year. Throughout this book, we have explored the use of authentic, digitised and inclusive assessments. In the coming chapters, we will look at the impact of feedback and feedforward, as well as how innovative assessment design can enhance learning with the added benefit of reducing academic misconduct.

As academics, standard questions asked by students include: 'Will this be in the assessment?', 'What will the exam questions be?' and 'What lecture slide will answer question X?' Such questions can be a real frustration for academics across the sector, particularly this over-emphasis on the end result at the expense of the richness of the educational experience. The resulting transactional attitude to Further and Higher Educational studies among students means that many may be less interested in learning than completing the necessary tasks that can be done, ticked off and that lead to the end result. Worryingly, since the government arguably turned students into consumers with the introduction of tuition fees (Dearing 1997), we have seen some concerning trends with students making demands regarding their attainment on the basis of paying for their education. Many academics will have had the unfortunate experience of being asked, 'I have paid a lot of money for this, why didn't I get a better grade?' This presents a challenge to all of those working in education who are driven by learning and arguably, the challenge is magnified when the final outcome of the course is not only a degree but a professional qualification. To put it bluntly, one would hope that student doctors were as knowledgeable about the areas of medicine that didn't happen to be the focus of an assessment as those that were; one would hope that student teachers were motivated to want to learn how best to help young learners to read, even if that particular area of professional knowledge was not the focus of a formal assessment.

There are parallels here with the surface-level learning Biggs and Tang (2011) refer to. The solution to this, it is argued, is to ensure that all elements of the offered curriculum are constructively aligned – intended learning outcomes, activities and assessment. This will lead to deeper learning. On a professional course, it is arguable that this alignment has to go further; alignment has to be made with the real world – the job. The challenge is to design assessment that is perceived as relevant and useful by the students. The cases in this chapter relate to primary student teachers. Our experiences suggest to us that student teachers may not always see the link between university-based training (and associated assessments) and the classroom. An oft-cited response from students demonstrating surface-level learning is, 'I'm alright in the classroom', thus suggesting a performative approach towards teaching and a failure to see links between subject knowledge and professionalism.

Professional courses, at both undergraduate and postgraduate level, are assessed both in the workplace and at the academic level. Certainly, this is true of teacher-education (training) courses (the differences here in language – education or training – betray a well-trodden debate about the nature of professional courses in this field). Students – trainees – are assessed on their practice as well as their knowledge and understanding of the theory and research underpinning this practice. Arguably, it is the latter, combined with the experiences allowed by the former, that informs professional judgement. Yet Knight (2013) points to a number of international studies which indicate the overwhelming value student teachers place on their school-based experience compared with university-based learning. Interestingly, this view aligns itself nicely to that of Gove's view of teaching (as Secretary of State for Education), as a craft, best learned *on-the-job*. While there can be no substitute for school-based experience, it is arguable that on its own it is not enough. The same conclusions could also be drawn from the earlier mentioned student doctors, in that it is important to gain experience in a medical setting but without the underpinning of prior medical research and theories of human biology, a future doctor would not have the fundamental knowledge necessary to undertake their role competently. In fact, this argument could apply to many professionals in society – engineers, lawyers, economists, scientists.

Classrooms are amongst the most complex working environments in which any professionals have to operate (Dudley 2010). Student teachers working in this environment learn to make decisions, to respond, to survive. They learn the ways of their particular school and class, the needs of their particular learners and the whims of their particular mentor. What they may not necessarily do is learn about learning. Hascher *et al.* (2004) remind us that practical experience may not be the same as learning. Doing is not the same as understanding why something worked – or didn't work – or questioning what it means in the classroom when something has worked. In order to be a true professional, student teachers need to do more than mimic. Professional knowledge and understanding must be transferrable and has to be embedded on firmer ground than experience. By its very nature, professionalism (and we argue that teaching is a profession not a craft) is concerned with a body of knowledge and a desire to be well-versed in it, to use knowledge to inform practice and, ideally, to contribute to its ongoing development. Such principles are embedded in professional, statutory and regulatory bodies (PSRB), where professional knowledge, practice and behaviours are lauded and valued. If these things are what it means to become and be a professional, then performative, surface-level practice just won't do and assessment – aligned to other components – must serve to foster deep learning and should persuade the learner of the importance of the bigger picture.

With the shift in culture and practice towards school-based training, the task for those of us working in Higher Education is further complicated. The busyness and complexities of working environments force students to contextualise, generalise and prioritise the here and now. Workplaces can seem remote and distant from research as decisions are made in the moment. Arguably, then, it becomes increasingly important for Higher Education providers to provide opportunities to prepare for the workplace and provide opportunities to reflect on practice, as both allow the student professional to step away from their particular context. Several questions may be raised here. How should we devise university-based training and associated assessment that has strong links to both the classroom and educational research without being watered down into top tips? How do we maintain the integrity of a Higher Education qualification that requires students to respond to summative assessments while designing the assessments in such a way that they develop students' understanding of and preparation for the real world, thereby allowing students to see the point of their assessments? How can we overcome the scepticism reported by many students about the value of research findings and theory in everyday classroom practice, which Knight (2013: 45) describes as notoriously difficult?

These are important questions. Research into students' perceptions of assessment show that they value assessment which they consider to have authentic value and prepare them for the workplace (Struyven *et al.* 2005). It is further argued that such assessments will encourage them to engage in deep learning (Brown 2004). The nature of the assessment and what makes it authentic may vary according to the discipline and the student body (Iannone and Simpson 2017) but, it is argued, authentic assessment goes a long way to helping to achieve these things. The concept of *authentic learning* is not new. The early 1970s, Freire discussed the importance of authentic learning, and asserted that authenticity is most important at assessment points (e.g. Freire 1970). It would seem, then, to be absolutely vital that we develop these opportunities, both for the importance of genuine learning and also for our students to see the value and purpose of these assessments in their journey to becoming qualified, ready to make professional judgements in whatever role they go on to fill.

Authentic assessment here is defined as 'the assessment of learning that is conducted through real world tasks requiring students to demonstrate their knowledge and skills in meaningful contexts' (Swaffield 2011: 434). As reflection is a key skill in many professions, the assessment can also involve reflecting on a real-world task. One of the tensions that is encountered in devising and using assessments based on real-world tasks is that students' experiences may differ widely. Placement contexts are various and multifaceted, so call for a situated pedagogy. In our case, as academics teaching teachers, we need to develop assessments that bridge the gap between the 'situation-specific knowledge' (Bloomfield *et al.* 2004: 359) that qualified and experienced teachers have and upon which they draw in the classroom on a day-to-day basis, and the professional body of knowledge that our student teachers gain throughout their years of study with us. In doing this, we are aware that our students are drawing on experiences in settings that are sometimes extremely varied and therefore providing them with contrasting approaches upon which to reflect and link to their professional understanding. Conversely, it could be said that this contrast is actually good for the students in terms of the varied experiences they have and how this prepares them for teaching. For us as academics and assessors, it can present tensions in terms of designing assessments that are equitable for students, whose opportunities to carry out the required tasks in such a way that they can provide effective material for reflection may be affected by the diverse nature of placement schools.

It is acknowledged that for some (Sambell *et al.* 2013; Mumm *et al.* 2016), authentic assessment cannot be demarcated from assessment *for* learning. The latter concept was used by Mumm *et al.* (2016), who outlined six key practices:

- Authentic assessment
- Balancing summative and formative assessment
- Creating opportunities for practice and rehearsal
- Designing formal feedback to improve learning
- Including opportunities for informal feedback
- Developing students as self-assessors

The design of assessments, outlined as case studies in this chapter, have proved more challenging than others simply because as academics, we have to work within the infrastructure and regulations of the university. Across the sector, academic regulations often inhibit the design of innovative and authentic assessment. Modular, credit-based structures restrict more holistic approaches as do rules stated by PSRBs. We also frequently face barriers in making changes to assessment in the lengthy lead times required for approval.

Case study 10.1: Assessment as a learning trap

Colette Ankers de Salis and Christine Smith, Liverpool John Moores University

Drawing on Biggs and Tang's principle of 'constructive alignment' (2011), we designed a level four module that aims to develop student teachers' subject knowledge of systematic synthetic phonics, curriculum knowledge, their pedagogical knowledge (how to teach this) and their skills of reflection. The learning is housed within an authentic experience that also marries Sambell *et al.*'s (2013) key practices: authentic assessment; balancing summative and formative assessment; creating opportunities for practice and rehearsal; designing formal feedback to improve learning; including opportunities for informal feedback; and developing students as self-assessors. The module prepares students for an authentic work-based experience that involves groups working together to plan and then teach phonics in school; the format is based loosely on the lesson-study approach. University-based sessions prepare them for the experience by developing subject, pedagogical and curriculum knowledge and by guiding them through the planning and reflection processes in lectures and workshops.

Following the university input, students work in groups of five. As a group, they plan together and 'take over' the phonics teaching in one class for a week. Each day, one person from the group assumes the role of the teacher. The rest of the group observes. After each lesson, the group gives feedback using guidance prompts. The 'teacher' reflects and the whole group decide if any changes need to be made to the following day's lesson. This aligns with developing students as self-assessors; providing opportunities for practice and rehearsal – students practise their planning and teaching of phonics – which in itself is not formally assessed here, though it is during their formal teaching practice; and providing opportunities for informal feedback from peers and formal feedback from observing teachers and/or university tutors.

Students are afforded the opportunity to rehearse and practise their fledgling planning skills: they attend guided planning workshops where videos of lessons are used to exemplify teaching and as prompts for discussion; students are invited to consider 'what the teacher was thinking?' at the planning stage and plans are modelled. Students are also invited to bring draft plans to another workshop. There they have the opportunity to ask questions, discuss their ideas and respond to formative verbal feedback. There is time for them to make changes to plans before they are required to teach. As the students are at level four, they will have had very limited experience in school. Moreover, our baseline assessment tells us that phonics is an area in which they lack confidence and subject knowledge. The university-based sessions develop subject, curriculum and pedagogical knowledge through lectures and workshops, which involve opportunities for peer and tutor informal feedback. For example, workshops include group tasks and students are invited to feed back to the group. This presents opportunities for questioning and clarification by both students and tutors. In terms of subject knowledge, there are informal assessments and self-assessment opportunities.

The summative assessment requires students to reflect on what they have learned about their teaching, drawing on their school and module experience. To support them with this, the concept of reflection is explored and linked to the notion of being a professional. Video footage of both phonics lessons and of former students reflecting are used in sessions.

This assessment aims to 'trap' students in their learning (students who do not attend and engage with all sessions struggle – there is no single assessment session) and encourage them to engage in deeper learning by making the experience authentic and relevant. We have had this in place for a number of years now and although we have made refinements and changes through our own reflection, in essence it has changed very little. Feedback from students about the nature of the assessment is consistently positive, with the overwhelming majority stating that it helps them in the classroom.

This assessment asks students acting in the role of teacher, to reflect upon action, after the event and those observing to also reflect in-action (Schön 1983). The problem we have with this module is that we are working with level four students who, as stated earlier, have very limited practical experience and recently acquired subject knowledge. Their tacit knowledge is therefore lacking – but we all need to start somewhere.

Authentic assessment may well encourage students to develop deeper learning in a real-world setting, but it also sees a shift from traditional forms of assessment. For many years, there has been an overreliance on linear testing in the form of end-of-term exams or the coursework standard of an essay. In Further Education, with the assessments set by an examination board, there is little room for any flexibility. In Higher Education, however, there is more freedom to be experimental (within academic regulations!). One only has to look at the impact of COVID-19 to see how quickly previously rigid structures can change, even PSRBs relaxed their rules around exams. The previous arguments for traditional assessments are going to be far tougher to maintain in the future.

Assessment robots

Tests and examinations are well known for testing lower-order thinking skills (Villarroel *et al.* 2019). Through such assessment mechanisms, students become passive learners that memorise information rather than fully comprehend it. Students can be quick to forget memorised content once the exam is completed (Rawson *et al.* 2013); it also leads to an approach to learning which is mechanical and not helpful in preparing a student for the more complex demands placed upon them in their roles beyond graduation. Skills such as reflection, collaboration, critical think ing, decision-making, problem-solving and communication are all key competencies which are not easily assessed in an exam. Within some subject areas, exams may still be relevant. In our earlier example of a student doctor, some information will need to be memorised – one would hope it is not something forgotten quickly!

Essays also fall within traditional assessment methods, arguably still a rigorous way of assessing academic scholarship, yet hardly ever a feature of life after college or university. It seems that essays only belong in academia. Essays are prone to academic misconduct and are labour-intensive to mark. Students tend to approach an essay with the assumption that there must be a correct answer and ask frustrating questions in an attempt to 'second guess' the lecturer: 'Where can I find the answer to this question?' Students become disempowered as learners. Assessment variety would show potential employers that graduates have a range of talents (MacAndrew and Edwards 2002). Our second case study explores how traditional forms of assessment can be replaced with an authentic assessment which replicates a skill which is required of graduates in their future role, that of a teacher.

Case study 10.2: Assessing authentic learning

Colette Ankers de Salis and Christine Smith, Liverpool John Moores University

Authentic assessments can sometimes be seen as taking the form of tasks that reflect those that our students will continue to experience once they are qualified and working. It is common for our students (once qualified) to be asked to present to their colleagues or to governors of their school around areas for school development for which they are responsible. Hence, we see presentations as a valid form of authentic assessment, and we use these across a variety of modules.

MacAndrew and Edwards (2002) argue for the place of assessments that link students' degree performance and their future employment. Another way in which this can be seen as an example of authentic assessment is that, in linking specifically to the individual student's placement tasks and experiences, the likelihood of plagiarism or any form of cheating is reduced to virtually nil. Where tensions may arise for such an assessment is in the area of equity of experience and what the placement provides for our student teachers in terms of material to reflect upon: Bloomfield et al.'s (2004: 358) 'complexity and diversity of placement contexts'. This is something we are keenly aware of and we work hard to ensure that all stakeholders are fully informed from the outset of the details of this assessment and its importance to students' degree outcomes, in order to enable students the best possible chances of success. As a real-world assessment, student feedback regularly shows that they see the value of this assessment; outcomes have been consistently good as a result.

This module includes a series of guest speakers, 'experts' or key practitioners in their fields of working with children with specific learning needs. This is designed to cover the range of additional needs students are likely to meet in the mainstream classroom. After a series of lectures and workshops with the various speakers, the students have a placement-related set of tasks to complete, where they focus on a pupil in their placement class who has a specific learning need that requires additional provision to enable them to be fully included in learning and make appropriate progress. This is deliberately kept open-ended, since it is not possible to be aware of the varied needs they will encounter until they actually begin their placement – and this occurs some weeks after the module delivery is completed, another example of the constraints of working with a modular system.

Students are scaffolded in terms of being given two explicit tasks that are designed to enable them to find out the relevant information they need to begin to meet the requirements of the assessment. This includes meeting with the school's Special Educational Needs Coordinator and discussing school policy and practice and how that links to national policy requirements. They then meet with their class teacher (their mentor) and discuss the specific needs of the pupils in the class, deciding collaboratively on a pupil on whom the student teacher will focus. As some classes may not have any pupils with diagnosed specific learning needs, the students are informed that they can choose any child with a differentiated need for whom the teacher has to make some additional provision. This is intended to make the assessment as equitable as possible and take account of the diverse nature of placements.

The core of the assessment is next comprised of the student observing the focus pupil over the course of a week – both in and out of the classroom context; again this is an example of authentic learning, as this will be an experience they will become increasingly familiar with and will find increasingly powerful as they continue with their professional development. They then design a series of three tasks/learning activities to enable the pupil to begin to overcome their barriers to learning. Their actual assessment focuses on them presenting a short overview of the initial placement tasks described above in order to contextualise their reflections, and then a reflection upon the learning activities they designed and the impact they had. Links can be seen here to the research quoted earlier from Mumm et al. (2016), as our students are developing themselves as self-assessors here. This task is often a powerful and quite formative experience for them in enabling them to reflect on their ability to enable pupils with specific barriers to overcome those barriers and make some progress.

Students who do not attend and engage with all sessions can sometimes struggle with this assessment, as they will have missed expert content and workshop learning that would enable them to effectively engage with the barriers their focus pupil may present. As they do not know what this specific need will be until after the module concludes and they begin their placement, they cannot select what content to attend and engage in but must instead engage with the whole module delivery. They do seem to recognise the value of this assessment though, and feedback is generally around how much they enjoyed having a module that linked very clearly to their placement experiences and scaffolded their developing understanding while on placement, by giving them focused stages to progress through and a clear outcome and goal to plan and aim for. As the presentations are carried out in small groups where each individual presents for ten minutes to a tutor and a small group of peers, with questions for five minutes at the end, the presentation process itself becomes a learning process for the audience; the varied needs they meet and contexts they work in provide a rich source of insight for the audience to take away themselves and reflect upon or look into further.

Handing over control

A key advantage of authentic assessment is that it is student focused, for it is they who will decide what approach they will take and how to present the information. Students must take ownership of their own knowledge to be successful (MacAndrew and Edwards 2002) and to embed the knowledge in a meaningful way. Such an approach may limit the temptation to plagiarise given that students are focusing on a unique situation – misconduct may require more effort than completing the assignment themselves – although it is not a complete deterrent (Ellis *et al.* 2019). It can be somewhat more complex to mark, which is often the argument levelled against authentic assessment. The assessment criteria are harder to design for with no set questions or a model answer; academics need to fully comprehend the submission as opposed to a standardised response to a uniform question.

Villarroel *et al.* (2019) suggest an authentic assessment cycle with three key phases and elements. Throughout this book, we have explored a number of these elements within the case studies presented.

Before – Plan authentic assessment

- Assessing what really matters
- Injecting realism into assessment
- Assessing complex thinking

During – Administer assessment in an authentic way

- Using open book tests
- Permitting collaborative answers
- Simulating realistic professional settings

After – Authentic feedback strategies

- Students develop marking criteria
- Students engage in peer review
- Using self-assessment in judging students' own work

This cycle, which provides some practical approaches to designing an authentic assessment that focuses on solving realistic problems and promotes the use of higher-order thinking skills, will go some way to better preparing students for life beyond graduation. We should be encouraging both convergent (closed) and divergent (open) thinking when we design our assessments. It is easier to assess convergent thinking, but a creative, divergent answer is more challenging (Guilford 1967).

If you are thinking after reading this chapter that more variety in assessment is necessary, please proceed with caution. Before introducing students to a different type of assessment, they need to have developed the skills to achieve in that assessment. If we take the example of a presentation as in Case Study 10.2, students are required to develop the performative skills required when presenting. Another increasingly common assessment is in the development of a poster. If you have developed an academic poster before, you will know that the effort required in formatting and designing it can outweigh the information you are attempting to portray. One of the key findings of the HEA-funded, Transforming the Experience of Students through Assessment project (TESTA 2015), was that too much variety leads to students focusing on the *what* rather than the *why*. We must ensure that the students have the opportunity to hone their skills. An example of this can be seen in the requirement of final-year students to submit an assessment poster. Being the first time in their studies that they had to produce one, it resulted in an undue amount of pressure and stress. We must allow students to develop their skills over a longer period of time, for repeating an assessment type provides the opportunity for students to test their skills, receive feedback and test them again. This is particularly important where the skills tested are likely to be required in their profession after university. A good example here is the use of presentations as assessments – students should be able to present at each level of study in order to receive feedback and develop confidence in their ability to present to a wider audience.

Key takeaways

An over-emphasis on the end result tends to place learning secondary to the assessment, thus developing a surface rather than deep learning approach on the part of our students. We need to reset the expectations of students to avoid passive and mechanical learning and to empower them to take control and ownership of knowledge. Assessment tasks should require an active demonstration of knowledge, instead of just writing an essay (Biggs and Tang 2011); they should go further than asking students to tell us what they know. Learners frequently seek the right answer, yet we need to prepare them for the fact that there may not be a single solution. Through this approach, students will develop the confidence and skills to deal with ambiguity and complexity. We need to develop authentic assessments that are based upon real-world experiences rather than encouraging students to mimic what we teach. For those students in the early stages of their Further or Higher Education, the real world may seem like a long way off, but the development of the skills they will need is vital. These skills should be practised throughout each level of study to provide the opportunity for students to receive and act upon feedback. It is important that a course/programme view is taken for coherence and to avoid over-assessment.

There are still barriers in place which restrict the development of more innovative assessments, yet the COVID-19 pandemic is an example of an event which forces the breaking down of these barriers by PSRBs, examination bodies and university regulations. We should ensure that we develop our approaches to assessment in a way which puts pressure on those seeking to revert back to traditional methods in the future.

Inspired by this chapter? Why not try ...

- *reviewing tests and examinations – are they the best way of assessing the knowledge and comprehension in your subject area?*
- *conducting a programme/course-wide audit of assessment – TESTA (2015) provides a useful methodology for conducting such a review*
- *developing 'live' assessments with external stakeholders to help bring the real world to life for students*
- *empowering students to support assessment design, perhaps even getting them to write the criteria by which they will be assessed*

11 Innovative assessment: Feeding back, feeding forward

To set the scene, imagine that you are working on a production line. At predictable, periodic intervals, a task is put in front of you. Your orders are clear, the end result has been clearly explained to you and the penalties for not completing the task have been outlined. All around you, other workers are similarly fixated on what needs to be done, all conscious that if they successfully complete the tasks assigned to them, the promised end result will be delivered. In this example, the end result would tend to be monetary in nature and would be the source of your motivation for working. Each task you complete acts as a stepping stone to your end goal and whilst you feel no particular connection to any part of the process, you approach each task with a degree of vigour that is linked to both the promise of an end result and also the consequences of non-compliance.

In his seminal book *Working for Ford*, Huw Beynon talks about the complete primacy of the production line and how workers are inducted into this instrumental view of work from the start. An oft-repeated phrase is that the 'line never stops' (Beynon 1975), whilst another common theme is the power struggle that exists between those working the line and those organising the line. The relationship between the two is viewed as transactional in nature. Those seen to be 'in charge' set the tasks and despite any unhappiness, resentment or disenfranchisement felt by those working the line, they comply as their focus is on what they will receive at the end of the process.

This focus on the end result is something that resonates within the current UK education system. Coffield and Williamson (2011) describe how the language of business has permeated every part of the sector and how the emphasis has shifted from the richness of the educational experience to the end result.

The emphasis amongst politicians is towards '"raising standards', by this term they mean nothing more than raising the test scores of students in a limited number of subjects' (Coffield and Williamson 2011: 2). As with our production line, participants in the process become used to delivering an end product. Their role is to complete tasks and if each is done to a satisfactory standard, then the end goal will be fulfilled. In both examples, an instrumentalist approach (Ade-Ojo and Duckworth 2015) has been enshrined in the process and has been adopted by participants.

Now, we need to move away from our production line to the process of painting a portrait. Here the focus moves away from a series of tasks, to the overall picture that should be kept in mind at all times. Every action will be designed to create something that is more than merely the sum of its parts. What has also changed is the nature of the relationship between the participants. In *The Picture of Dorian Gray*, Oscar Wilde described the process thus: 'Every portrait that is painted with feeling is a portrait of the artist, not of the sitter' (Wilde 1890) – in other words, there has been a shift in the power dynamics. Instead of a transactional relationship, there is a relationship that could be described as transformational in nature. Both parties are fully invested in the process and the result is that instructional tasks are replaced by the realisation that continuous thought and reflection can produce something that manifests the journey the participants have undertaken.

The advent of mass participation in UK Further and Higher Education that was precipitated by the Further and Higher Education Act 1992 has had a number of consequences that have altered the relationship that students have with their assessment during their studies. Foremost amongst these has been a shift from autonomy to regulation through the sector, with checks on quality becoming increasingly common. These checks include the creation of the Quality Assurance Agency (QAA), whose remit is to safeguard standards and improve standards in Higher Education (QAA 2019) and Ofsted, whose aim is to ensure that 'organisations providing education, training and care services in England do so to a high standard for children and students' (Ofsted 2019). In addition, there are a multitude of other quality checks which measure aspects such as the quality of teaching, the quality of research and each organisation's engagement with groups who have had traditionally lower participation rates in Further and Higher Education. Each of these checks leads to the bestowing of a quality award, a published report or a league table that ranks the organisation.

This increased regulation, coupled with the increased fees students pay for their Higher Education studies, has created a sector where the balance between lecturer and students has shifted. Whilst the relationship is not quite that of an organisation with its customers, the shift has created 'student-consumers' (Tomlinson 2017), who are looking at their education experience as an opportunity to achieve a qualification rather than merely seeing it as an end in itself. This instrumental approach to their studies has been reinforced by a compulsory sector that focuses on (and is measured by) exam results and the end product of students' studies.

The result of a culture that is characterised by quality checks and students who are viewed as consumers, by assessment and feedback and feedforward, has been an innate conservatism. Colleges and universities have taken to creating module information documents that detail exactly what students can expect from any given part of the course and lecturers are instructed not to deviate from the information provided. Whilst this does create a more homogeneous approach, its rigidity means that participants view the experience in transactional terms. Just like our production line, there is a known input and if all procedures are followed, there will be a known output.

Assessment as a driver for student learning

This approach also feeds into the assessment of learning. The view of Race (2014) that assessment should be the major driver for student learning is a widely held viewpoint, yet in many organisations, assessment is not treated in this way. The standard approach used is that the content of the module is decided first and then assessment is added at the end. This assessment is often accompanied by a marking guide that signposts students to an approach which will result in a given mark. The actual assessment itself is often a reflection of the conservatism of the sector with essays, reports, exams and presentations being used in the vast majority of cases. Whilst these can be valid forms of assessment, the tendency with each of them is to validate that learning has taken place, rather than be used as a major driver for future student learning. In addition to this, the disconnect between the assessment and the learning that occurs when assessment is added to the module rather than being the focal point for the module, encourages students to view assessment as a task to be completed rather than an integral part of the learning process. This is reinforced by their lack of involvement in the creation of the tasks and the tendency amongst lecturers to explain *what* is needed for each part of the assessment rather than *why* it takes place.

As we can see from our first case study, some organisations have taken steps to address this and also the worry that students often attach to assessment.

Case study 11.1: Involving students in assessment design

Natalie Morris, Access to HE, Bedford College

Summative assessment can sometimes feel like an insurmountable problem for students. Not only is there a lot at stake, but it's often cited as being confusing, especially for students who are moving to a new phase of their education journey. During a conversation at the end of one of my lessons, one student likened it to 'throwing a dart whilst blindfolded'. Another said, 'you never know what the next teacher will want'. Some students describe the feeling of being 'exposed' when handing in an assessment, which is only exacerbated if they aren't clear about what they are being judged against.

Clearly, this highlights issues with the way assessments are being communicated to students and it is not conducive to optimal performance. This discussion led to a renewed focus on assessment and the piloting of more involvement from students in shaping the assessments.

The Access to Higher Education course has traditionally experienced high levels of resubmissions. In 2015–16, up to 50% of students were asked to resubmit work early in the course. The data shows that it is largely the same students that are still being asked to resubmit at the end of the course (in 2015–16, 25% were asked to resubmit their third assessment). During resubmission, they are asked to add to their work and hand it in again, which increases workload for students that are already finding the course hard. It also significantly increases the marking for teachers.

I reflected on why this could be happening and decided to start a pilot study with a relatively small group of 15 Access to Teacher Education students. All pathways receive a basic introduction to expectations for assessment at the college and a run-through of their assignment briefs but other than that, support for assessment is individual to each teacher; some do more than others. Whilst thinking about this, I noticed that the curriculum for this group does not currently contain anything about assessment. I realised I could address both of these issues by involving students in designing their own assessments. The aim of this was to enrich their curriculum by exposing them to the theory and practice of assessment and to improve their confidence and understanding of their own assessments. Ideally, it would also make assessment more interesting.

The process involved four distinct stages:

Teaching them about assessment

Students had a session looking at what assessment is, issues with assessment (e.g. accessibility and validity) and also covered how assessment needs to be used to judge the level of the work. It was important to have any grade descriptors, or other grading information, available at this point and actually studying the purpose of assessments caused plenty of 'lightbulb' moments for students.

Set boundaries

Boundaries for the student-designed assessment were made clear early on to prevent confusion (or over-excitement). I asked everyone to agree to one assessment to reduce complications with submission and marking. I also make it clear that I have the final decision on the assessment, even though they are involved in the design. For example, when they decided they wanted to make short videos, I reviewed the method, wrote the assignment brief, decided where and how submission would take place, made arrangements for IT equipment to be available for all students, organised IT support, etc.

Get creative

We start with a no-holds-barred mind map of any and every assessment method they can think of – no matter how unusual. I even had interpretive dance as a suggestion! The map was put on the board and when all ideas were exhausted, we went through them one at a time to begin elimination. Students decide which ones to keep, and which ones don't meet the needs of the assessment (e.g. not accessible to all). From this point, I would normally go one of two ways, depending on the nature of the group; I either set it as homework that they collaborate as a group and bring one method to me or I ask them to vote. Each method has its pros and cons and will be better suited to different groups of students.

Polish

All that's left is to 'polish' and make sure it works with our submission systems, referencing policies and quality systems. At this point, the assignment brief can be written and any teaching that may be required for that assessment method can be planned.

Having used this method for the last two years, the key points to remember are as follows:

- Make the boundaries of the activity really clear. Decide what you feel comfortable with and what you are able to offer to the students in advance of discussing it with them
- Allow plenty of time in class as well as outside of class for your and their planning around this. It does take a bit more time, but less time than all the remarking
- This activity is all about transparency. If there is an assessment method you are ruling out, explain why. It will only deepen their understanding of assessment methods. If this is because of it being too time-intensive for you, it's okay to say that! I find that explaining these things to them helps them to understand the sheer volume of marking (and everything else) I have and only increases the respect between us
- Once students have a better understanding of why assessment takes place, how it works and what they need to do to be successful at it, they grow in confidence with increased pass rates

The results of using this method have been extremely positive. Students have praised this method to external verifiers and it was also passed onto the awarding body Quality Managers who tried it in the classroom and reported back to us that, 'It works!' This endorsement is backed up by the change in the number of resubmissions in each module that has used this approach. Every single assessment has significant drops in resubmissions as students engage in the process far more and understand what the purpose is.

What Natalie has described is a collaborative approach that moves away from the transactional approach to assessment that has become prevalent. Students can not only see the purpose of what they are doing but they are also co-constructors of the approach, which creates not only a better understanding of the process but a far greater commitment to the assessment due to their role in its evolution. Instead of being an 'add-on' to the module, it becomes an essential part of the learning process.

Engaging with assessment

Once the assessment has been completed and marked, a new challenge emerges. The transactional nature of much of the assessment encourages students to move on to the next task rather than to reflect on what has been learnt. Research shows that whilst over 90% of undergraduate students access their marks, only a quarter of level 4 students do the same with their feedback and feedforward (Wolstencroft and de Main 2020). In part, this can be put down to the variable nature of the comments made; bland, generic comments that merely rank the assessment within a hierarchy, such as 'good work' or 'covers all criteria' are unlikely to elicit much engagement, but mostly the lack of interest students have in the comments can be said to be due to their view of assessment as a set of tasks (Ali *et al.* 2017).

This instrumental approach to their assessment means that once something has been completed to their satisfaction, the task is viewed as complete. Other than a minority of students who do access and explore the comments written, it is only if something does not align with students' expectations that they fully engage with what has been written. Whilst in part it can be argued that students are rarely trained in how to use feedback and feedforward in subsequent assignments (San Pedro 2012), it might also be argued that the approach used by most colleges and universities encourages this approach.

Whilst the provision of detailed assessment briefings encourages students to follow a set pattern, the widespread use of anonymised marking and electronic platforms for comments can create the feeling for students that assessment is disconnected from the rest of their studies. Markers cannot see whose work they are assessing and students are often unaware who has graded their work. Instead, pre-stored comments and generic rubrics justify grades whilst there are often few comments that are personalised to students. This justification for the grading approach feeds the narrative that if students follow a set of instructions, then the end result is the inevitable consequence.

Whilst the way in which students perceive induction, transitions and support in education has been extensively researched (Wilcox *et al.* 2012), students' attitudes to feedback have received much less attention. What research that has been conducted has found that where comments are personalised, engagement is far higher. Whilst this might seem obvious, actually making sure that it happens is rather more problematic. The reasons for this are many and include the number of scripts and timescale in which they need to be marked for assessors, the encouragement towards uniformity of assessment, and the fact that any challenge to the current status quo tends to be faced with resistance from both students and staff.

The use of innovative approaches in this area often depends on the students' view of the process. If the problem is merely a lack of understanding of how it works and how one assignment is part of a wider landscape, then the answer can be found in educating students to fully engage. However, in other cases, a change to a differing approach to assessment can be beneficial, as we see in our second case study.

Case study 11.2: Video as an alternative to written assessment and feedback

Kay Calver and Fran Hall, BA Childhood and Youth Studies, University of Northampton

We selected a level four module that revolved around the acquisition of study skills, alongside considering definitions of childhood and youth as well as what it means to be a young person. The assessment asked the students to create an e-portfolio using EduBlogs software, where each section addressed a different aspect of the module. The idea was to bring together a range of multi-media techniques for the students and get them to engage in quite high-level techniques to develop their digital literacy skills. A lot of the students felt apprehensive about doing a video as part of their EduBlog, so given that we asked students to capture themselves on film, we thought that we should demonstrate this ourselves, and we decided to use a video format. A summative feedback video was recorded for each student talking through each aspect of their portfolio and then we talked through their overall strengths and weaknesses before giving their final grade at the end. This video was then embedded into their EduBlog for students to access. No written comments were given.

Students appreciated this approach, as we pitched it to show we were modelling things in our own practice. They viewed it as fair, as we were not asking them to do something we wouldn't do ourselves. As part of the video (using the Kaltura system), we tracked how long they watched it for and how many times they accessed their feedback and then carried out a focus group and sent questionnaires to the students about their experiences. What we found is that the majority said they don't read written feedback at all. They just look at the grade, which was rather disheartening. However, what we found was that they engaged in the video far more. Part of this was undoubtedly because we told them the grade at the end of the video and we didn't put their grade anywhere else until a week later, so if they wanted the grade on time, they had to access the video but there was also the sense that they wanted to hear what we had to say about their work. One point to note is that some of them did say that they skipped to the end of the video, as they were anxious about the grade so they couldn't digest the feedback until they knew how they had done.

Recording the feedback was a different experience but we really liked it. Being captured on film was not always comfortable but it was much more personalised for the student. Our worry with written feedback was that it could be interpreted in different ways. Students found that they could understand the message more easily if they could see us, as we could present things in a more supportive way. We found that we could say a lot more and we gave a lot more feedback in the video. Looking back, as it was a big assignment (3000-word equivalent), we gave 8–10 minutes of feedback but the students said that was too long, and so when we do it again, we will reduce it to three minutes. We thought the students would love more feedback but they said that they got bored and switched off before the end, so three minutes is probably ideal. We found that incredible as we imagined that they would want to improve. Even though myself and Fran had taught them all term and we were giving them specific examples of how they could improve, they still got bored by the end of the video.

A lot of the students loved the personalised approach, although those that had not done as well as they expected found it too personalised. They found it difficult to watch, as they felt embarrassed and they felt that they had been told off. Despite the fact that we presented it in a really supportive manner, because we were looking at them and talking to them, they struggled. As it was a Year 1 module, they hadn't had much feedback and that is an issue; when we do it again, we need to prepare students to engage in constructive criticism. They also mentioned our use of language. Many students were looking out for words such as 'however' or 'but', as they knew that when we said that, we were about to turn and talk about something not so good. It is normal for us to do this but for them they were waiting for the turn.

We would love to do this again, building on this experience, but it is not for everyone. There is a need for good digital literacy skills and the confidence to do something different. Doing something new or different for some members of staff can be overwhelming but it does work. We use a lot of audio feedback, as students enjoy that and engage with it. It also means that you can personalise it rather more easily. Video feedback takes this even further.

A key change outlined in this case study is the way in which the process of assessing learners has been altered to reflect the relationship between student and lecturer. Whilst the idea of the lecturer as a role model is an interesting one, it is the matching of the assessment approach to the feedback and feedforward used that stands out. This changes the relationship from one that is transactional to a more relationship-based model. The fact that students can see who is assessing them creates a degree of personalisation that alters assessment from something to be completed, to something that is part of an ongoing relationship with the tutor. The fact that some students, who did not do as well as they thought, felt embarrassed when watching the video, seems to indicate a degree of engagement that might not be present if they were merely handed written comments.

A further point highlighted by our second case study concerns the amount of feedback offered to students. A common complaint from students has been the generic nature of many comments but with a video and audio approach, far more can be communicated. Whilst this does not negate the problem of students fast forwarding to the end of the video, or indeed not accessing the video at all, it does mean that the combination of an increased amount of feedback and feedforward, the personalised approach and the established relationship that exists between students and staff, is likely to lead to a change in perception of the process.

This change is not without its problems and these can occur on both sides of the relationship. First, the approach requires a change in practice from members of staff, and at the outset the change might well seem like a 'leap into the unknown'. Video (or even audio) feedback is perceived to be more time-consuming and problematic than a traditional approach, yet the reality is the opposite. Whilst this problem can be overcome comparatively easily, the second issue is more difficult to solve. Given the focus on fixed, homogeneous, quality procedures within Further and Higher Education, the temptation amongst lecturers is to opt for a safe option that is not likely to be questioned by students. Often lecturers are evaluated by students and deviations from an expected approach can be perceived negatively by some classes.

The views of students also need to be modified in order to maximise the benefits of this approach. Engagement with assessment (and in particular feedback and feedforward) requires an iterative rather than instrumental approach. A degree of reflection, especially reflection 'on action' (Schön 1983), is needed and this means that the general focus on the grade rather than the comments needs to be changed. Given that the majority of students have been told of the primacy of their final grade, this can be a challenge; however, if a relationship can be built with the assessor, it is likely to be possible. More structured reflection in the first year of a course can be used to introduce the concept before a more nuanced (and individual) approach is used as students progress through their studies.

Key takeaways

Returning now to our original premise, it is easy to see how the approach adopted by many organisations to assessment and to feedback and feedforward can be likened to the repetitive tasks on a production line. As with Beynon's (1975) description, those at the centre of the process do not see the big picture, and instead focus solely on the task in front of them. Once they have completed it, they wait for the next task, which is approached with reference to clear instructions. The process is a linear succession of tasks and the degree of autonomy is minimal. Students have become used to focusing on an end result that is viewed by themselves (and others) as matching their expectations. As with our production line workers, if these expectations have been met, then they feel ready to move on to the next task. Whilst this approach is not without some merit, in that it encourages students to strive towards meeting the set standards, the lack of reference to the overall picture means that students are not aware of what they are working towards or indeed they fail to learn from each task, hence potentially causing stagnation and an instrumental approach that fails to build on lessons learnt previously.

The key goal of the innovative techniques discussed in this chapter is to encourage students, as well as members of staff, to move towards an approach more akin to that of a painter, whereby each task completed is set in the context of the bigger picture.

The benefits from this approach include the following:

- Each task completed is analysed to see how the next one can be improved, with the consistent objective of ensuring that the final result is as good as possible

- Assessment becomes integrated into the process of learning rather than merely being seen as an 'add on' to a module
- It can promote greater engagement in the learning process – students tend to be more interested, as it is a different approach from anything they have experienced previously
- It stops assessment becoming transactional in nature
- Assessment becomes personalised – students can see how they are being treated as an individual

There are challenges to adopting this approach:

- Changing anything is often viewed as a risk and may be met with some resistance
- Lecturers do need to set limits to the process
- It can be disorientating for students, as it is a different process to that which they are used to, and they often need more explanation and support
- It increases vulnerability, as students have to engage with their weaknesses as well as their strengths
- There can be a perception amongst staff that this approach requires additional time and resources

Whilst involving students in the design of the assessments and ensuring that modules include assessment at their core rather than an afterthought does help this process, it is when designing the feedback and feedforward that this approach becomes most crucial. Innovative techniques in this area look to engage students by personalising the process, building a relationship, encouraging critical reflection and instead of getting students to see assessments as goals to be achieved, getting them to see them as individual parts of a whole that they have far more autonomy over.

Inspired by this chapter? Why not try ...

- *using podcasts to give students information about their assessments*
- *trying to organise a webinar to support students with their work*
- *using audio/video feedback and feedforward*
- *releasing a student's grade after they have received the feedback comments*
- *using either self-reflection or peer reflection to get students to think about what they have written*

12 Innovative assessment: Authentic assessment to beat the cheats

TEF Principles this chapter refers to:

Teaching quality: teaching that stimulates and challenges students, and maximises engagement with their studies

Student outcomes and learning gain: the extent to which all students achieve their educational and professional goals, in particular those from disadvantaged backgrounds

Stand outside a campus for long enough and you might be approached by someone offering to 'help' you with your assignments –they may even hand you a card with their contact details. Perhaps you take to social media to express your anxiousness in completing an essay on time and within minutes an 'expert' reaches out to offer you some advice. These 'experts' can originate from freelance auction sites, essay mills and a variety of other sources. They have one thing in common: to profit from students willing to pay for someone else to write their assignments. It is plagiarism commercialised.

You can see how they operate for yourself by searching online for 'essay help' and viewing the large number of operators in the market. If you dare, try searching for your module/unit code or assignment title. Like many academics, you might even find that your assessments have already appeared online posted by students seeking help. It can be incredibly exasperating for an academic, particularly when you have dedicated hours to designing learning materials and supporting students. For a conscientious student, it invokes anger and frustration to learn that other students take the 'easy' route. Such students comment that it devalues their degree and spoils the feeling of success after their own hard efforts to then learn that others have got away with cheating. The price of written assessments can vary depending on the number of words, desired grade boundary and deadline. At the time of writing, a 3000-word, second-class assignment due in seven days would cost around £150, whilst a PhD thesis would cost around £2500 with a little more time allowed. Assignment providers use increasingly aggressive marketing techniques to persuade students that the service will support them. Draper and Newton (2017) investigated the terms and conditions of providers recognising that they shift the responsibility of 'fraud' to the student through the misuse of the product provided. They go on to suggest a legal approach focused on targeting the commercial providers of written assignments, although Amigud and Dawson (2020) question whether legal prohibition is even effective.

The buying of assessments, now recognised as *contract cheating*, was initially defined as 'the submission of work by students for academic credit which the students have paid contractors to write for them' (Clarke and Lancaster 2006). Lancaster (2018) provides further clarification:

"Contract cheating describes the process through which students can have original work produced for them, which they can then submit as if this were their own work. Often this involves the payment of a fee and this can be facilitated using online auction sites"

With the increased use of technology and electronic assessment submissions, it is now far easier for a student to access services and retrieve a completed essay than before. There is a great deal of anecdotal evidence that cases of contract cheating are on the rise, but it is not so simple to quantify. Universities can only report on cases they have detected, so a large number of students may slip through the net. Research conducted by Newton (2018) found that 15.7% of students admitted to paying for someone else to complete their work, potentially representing 31 million students globally. It was also established that there was a significant positive relationship between time and admission of guilt, suggesting that students do not own up until sometime after graduation once the risk of confessing is perceived to have faded.

Some studies have indicated that both students and academics have difficulties recognising traditional plagiarism (see Roig 2001; Glendinning 2014). To add to the complexity, unlike more traditional forms of academic misconduct, contract cheating cannot be detected using similarity software. It relies upon the detection skills of the academic marker and this often means that cases are dealt with quite differently. Common things to look out for include unusual references and citations, unusual writing style and not adhering to academic guidance provided. However, the sophistication of paid essay writers has evolved to anticipate these warnings with many mirroring the standard of prior work submitted. On occasion, the evidence is more forthcoming. There have been cases of students whistleblowing on peers, and certain document properties highlighting the author to be a known essay mill. There also appears to be a growing number of assignment writing organisations that are reporting to the student's college or university if payment for the service is not made. In many institutions, the penalty for students is extremely serious; with solid evidence, the student is likely to be permanently excluded.

Facilitated by technology, contract cheating has become more prominent in the last decade. However, traditional plagiarism has existed for centuries, for as long as there has been text to copy. With the widespread use of similarity software, plagiarism and collusion are somewhat easier to detect when compared with contract cheating. However, there are instances where students try to mask the plagiarism, such as through the use of white text or text as an image, which cannot be detected by software. In many cases, plagiarism is the result of poor academic referencing or a misunderstanding of how to cite the work of others. It is clear with contract cheating that the act of making a payment demonstrates deliberate, pre-planned intent.

In most cases of academic misconduct there are common factors that drive students to seek an alternative to completing the assignment themselves.

- *Lack of time*: Students have conflicting priorities which may stem from other assessment deadlines and undertakings such as work or social activities. Poor planning and time management may also result in leaving assessment writing until close to the deadline (see Park *et al.* 2013; Smith *et al.* 2013).
- *Lack of subject knowledge*: Students may struggle to understand learning materials provided. There may be personal and institutional barriers in place which prevent the student from seeking additional support.
- *Lack of academic writing skills*: This is more apparent in those students for whom English is a second language (see Ledesma 2011; Bretag *et al.* 2019). They may experience issues of confidence to write an academic assignment, which results in copying large amounts of text or buying work.

In more isolated cases, students do not intend to complete the work with integrity and from the outset plan to copy or buy their assignments. The call for a focus on academic integrity has grown in recent years. The International Center for Academic Integrity defines academic integrity as 'a commitment, even in the face of adversity, to six fundamental values: honesty, trust, fairness, respect, responsibility, and courage' (ICAI 2019). It is widely recognised that students cheat more than once during their studies (see Nonis and Swift 1998; Whitley 1998; Quintos 2017) and factors such as the likelihood of being caught, peer influence and the severity of the consequences have a critical role to play in influencing student behaviour (Brimble and Stevenson-Clarke 2005). With the high number of international students studying in the UK, there are differing attitudes towards copying the work of others; this must be recognised in the induction and development of students new to studying in the UK. Bretag (2018) explored a number of variables to identify who cheats: gender, age, academic discipline, language proficiency and academic ability. Overall, the results in general were mixed and inconclusive.

In our first case study, Judith explores an occurrence of misconduct during her teaching and reflects upon the incident and subsequent impact of changing practice.

Case study 12.1: Beating the cheats or supporting good academic practice?

Judith Darnell, Bedford College

This case study explores how one student made the decision to plagiarise an assignment whilst studying for the Educational Practice Foundation Degree. The incident occurred when I was relatively new to Higher Education teaching. I had fully discussed the dangers of plagiarism with the cohort of students from the outset. As part of the students' development, it was important for them to not only have experience reading academic texts but also to discuss and review excerpts of anonymised essays associated with different or old units (with the writers' permission). My intention was to use this material to highlight the successful use of academic tone, pinpoint the ways in which an argument can be formed and to explore correct and incorrect ways to reference material alongside the demonstration of educational subject knowledge. I was very careful to provide small excerpts and made it clear that these papers must be kept within the classroom and were for providing a platform for discussion and analysis only. However, during a break, one student returned to the classroom and covertly took photographs of the excerpts. The student then submitted an assignment that was remarkably similar to the examples provided. After much investigation, the student's actions were realised through self-admission, the penalty being a fail. The student was permitted a re-take the following year but was liable for tuition fees and had to cease study for ten months. The student had a good attendance record and although present during the sessions on plagiarism, referencing and study skills during the initial weeks of the course, had panicked on this occasion due to lack of confidence in finding appropriate sources, producing academic writing and using correct referencing formalities, although the student admitted that knowledge of the subject of the assessment had not troubled them.

After the incident, I took time to reflect and change my practice. In Higher Education, students must be aware that the route to a successful assessment is not all about subject knowledge. The skill of academic writing is a major component of the process of higher attainment. Successful academic writing relies upon a knowledge of structures, rules and tone that are, for the most part, gained and taught through reading other academic discourse. Students who are able to understand and follow the same rules for their own ideas, woven together using a highly organised referencing system, can achieve success. Not only is referencing important for avoiding plagiarism, it is fundamental in achieving the tone in which academic writing sits. Knowledge of the above was integral to thinking about how best to combat plagiarism within the Educational Practice course and was rooted in ensuring that students had the confidence and knowledge to understand the following:

- how academic writing is unique from other forms of writing
- the importance of robust information-searching and note-taking techniques

- that organisation plays a fundamental role in collecting and using correct references to their full effect
- that subject knowledge and study skills are not separate entities but need to be constantly applied and integrated alongside each other

Knowing that a student had copied the work from prior assignments might have initiated withdrawal of all examples of previous work being used in class. However, it was my feeling that providing an even larger 'example pool' of essays would not encourage plagiarism but would actually give more opportunity for the students to immerse themselves in academic writing style and would therefore heighten understanding of the different forms of sentence structure, tone and referencing. Students needed to be surrounded not only by academic literature but also by different examples of academic writing. To be submerged this way helped to ensure that students were able to take on the systems seen in other work. To know that a larger number of papers gained a 2:1 in different ways was a fundamental lesson in giving students confidence that there was not only one way to write to achieve highly. If they were able to find ways to adopt a similar academic writing style, then their ideas and own reading could just as successfully be woven to produce a unique piece. Lack of confidence through lack of submersion was considered one of the main triggers among students who plagiarised. Therefore, I approached this problem by:

1 Providing a wider range of examples of essays with varying grades whilst encouraging students to attempt to work out which essays achieved higher grades than others and to explore the reasons for this (note that although students could have ready access to these examples in class, they could not be photographed, taken home or copied from).
2 Frequently modelling techniques in class used for sourcing scholarly academic material using the online library and teaching the practical skills of note-taking.
3 Modelling or exploring aspects of referencing within every session and finding opportunities to check students' understanding through small group activities, peer discussion and use of examples. One of the most engaging activities I found was to display an incorrect reference, provide access to the source of that reference and to ask students to investigate the mistake that had been made.
4 Being very clear from the outset about plagiarism, explaining how and why students may be tempted to plagiarise, how plagiarism is detected and the consequences of such misconduct.

Integrating referencing with note-taking activities and academic writing skills into every session ensured that students were not segregating 'subject knowledge' and 'study skills' but combining them, the importance of which can be easily overlooked in education. Many institutions teach study skills and referencing in the first few weeks and expect students to grasp and use this newfound skill instantly. I found that it was more appropriate to revisit this frequently alongside the teaching of subject knowledge within the classroom. Students were more likely to ask questions, reflect, explore and analyse their work and writing styles with peers. This provided valuable opportunities

> to confront any misunderstandings before students were faced with an assignment and were tempted to plagiarise as a desperate and frantic reaction to uncertainties and lack of confidence.
>
> Using the philosophy described above, plagiarism cases reduced to zero and student success increased through higher than average outcomes across the groups, with many students achieving first-class assignments.

In this case study, Judith has identified some of the key drivers for academic misconduct mentioned above and has reflected on what measures can be taken to overcome them through alternative approaches to assessment preparation. Key to this experience was the lack of confidence displayed by students, particularly the student who made the ill-fated decision to copy the excerpts provided. The lack of subject knowledge here was not a concern, but the lack of academic writing skills may have influenced the student's actions. It is also evident that more organisation and structure, in this case through the use of note-taking, can assist students in better time management and developing their academic writing skills.

Prevention not detection

It is easy to be drawn into developing lengthy strategies on detecting contract cheating or plagiarism with a focus on disciplinary measures and academic penalties. Such an approach often involves a high demand on academic resources to investigate and conclude such incidents, and it is also an emotive activity for all involved. It may seem a simple solution to revert back to examination-based assessment in a reactionary move to prevent misconduct. However, the designing out of plagiarism opportunities in assessment is key in proactively reducing incidences of misconduct. In Chapter 10, we discussed authentic assessment and its importance in developing students' understanding. Using original assessments can also diminish the opportunities for students to avoid completing the assignment themselves.

In our second case study, Mark Sutcliffe shares some examples of authentic assessment through the use of artefacts.

> **Case study 12.2: Authentic assessment through the use of artefacts**
>
> *Mark Sutcliffe, Cardiff School of Management, Cardiff Metropolitan University*
>
> The Masters in International Business Management taught within Cardiff School of Management is a strongly student-centred programme of study that promotes active participation and engagement, and has a teaching and learning strategy that is focused upon problem-based learning. Since its

early inception, the programme has developed and used a range of artefacts, made objects (physical and digital) that have interest or significance attached to them or within them, to promote and consolidate teaching, learning and reflection.

The rationale behind getting students to create artefacts evolved from two related issues faced by the programme; the first concerned dealing with a highly diverse cohort of students, and the second was the desire to get post-graduate students to demonstrate deep understanding and sophisticated thinking, something not always possible through traditional assessment methods.

The Masters in International Business Management is a master's programme that typically has a cohort of between 30 and 40 students, who are drawn from a wide and varied global demographic. Many students have a background in business education, but not all, hence the cohort is both ethnically and academically diverse. It is critical for the success of the programme that this diversity and difference in recruitment should not become a barrier to learning, both academically and socially. The aim of the first artefact that was created, known as the Belonging Cube (discussed further below), was created to help decolonise the education experience (Ryan and Tilbury 2013) and allow students to share something of themselves with their peers in a way that was engaging, active and reflective. Artefacts that have been developed subsequently have had this element underpinning their creation, acting as a way to empower students, not only in creating content but in determining its subject matter and focus, providing an opportunity for personal and reflective outcomes. The creation of authentic assessment tasks aims to challenge students, to take them out of their comfort zone and require them to demonstrate 'deep understanding, higher order thinking, and complex problem solving through the performing of exemplary tasks' (Koh 2017). The issue is how best to do this, and how, at the same time, you might enhance student creative skills and promote a future-facing view of education, which taps into those capabilities and skills that students need in order to deal with uncertain outcomes and the security of current knowledge.

The Belonging Cube (the creation and application of this is well documented elsewhere; see Kneale 2015) proved to be a highly successful activity in helping to shape feelings of belonging and establish a community of practice. One of the main outcomes of the cube was to show to students that as diverse a group as they were, they in fact all shared the same hopes, fears and aspirations, and that they all belonged to a group and were not alone. The physical nature of the activity and how it was used to illustrate situations and context was so profound that it led to the development of other activities that involved encouraging students to create objects and shape content, in effect putting something of themselves into the artefact that they create, often reflecting either their cultural background and identity (e.g. The Transition Tube, augmented reality key rings, zines – online magazines, digital CVs) or their academic interests (The Scrapbook).

The Transition Tube. The Transition Tube, a reused snack container, was an artefact developed to allow students, at various transition points throughout the academic year, to provide content reflecting on their progress. The content took various forms, including the production of a skills newsletter, the creation of survival guidelines presented on a series of luggage labels, and the development of a feedforward questionnaire to evaluate assessment feedback. Eight tasks in total were included in the tube, the final one of which required students to decorate the tube based upon the theme of a 'journey' (a full review of the tube and the tasks included can be found in Matheson *et al.* 2018). The Transition Tube artefact, composed in and of itself of artefacts, was then gifted to new students arriving on the following year's programme, with the express aim of aiding the transition of the subsequent cohort. Along with a reflection on the purpose of the Transition Tube and the process of its creation, this work constituted the assessment for the student's professional development module. The tube acts as a physical time capsule, capturing transition as an emergent process throughout the year, requiring students to reflect upon their progress and consolidate their learning in the tasks required.

The Scrapbook. This artefact was developed in order to encourage creative and original thinking, empowering students to both select content and the way it is presented, breaking away from the traditional essay and its associated problems in establishing authenticity. Students are given a traditional blank scrapbook and instructed that they must select a contemporary issue in international political economy, and then over the year investigate this issue presenting the story using a variety of visual mediums, and using creative ways to show and display content, such as timelines, person/idea profiles or boxes, glossary, augmented reality (AR) content, QR codes, etc. The work is supported throughout the year with formative feedback templates at key points on specific aspects of the work: layout, content, and analysis and evaluation. In addition to good writing skills, students are challenged to show effective communication using a variety of visual media, and creative forms of presentation. No two scrapbooks are the same, and with effective task management in topic selection, every student is required to produce an original and creative piece of work.

The artefacts on the programme were not all created at a single point but instead developed and evolved year on year, and as they have developed and evolved so has their sophistication. In addition to encouraging students to explore their identity and interests, we now use artefacts as an opportunity to promote, develop and enhance skills, especially digital skills and in particular opportunities to use AR. For example, the zine (online magazine) required students to work in multicultural teams, discuss cultural difference in relation to an aspect of culture, such as food or fashion, and then write an article and create and embed within it an element of AR content exploring the cultural similarities and differences between them (social learning).

The artefact tasks can be assessed both formally and summatively in a variety of formats. Marking rubrics can be used to attempt to capture the complex content and creativity, but require careful consideration given the diversity of content that such artefacts tend to present. Artefacts do take students out of their comfort zone. They provide variety and originality in the learning, teaching and assessment diet, and offer a new and challenging way for staff to consider what students learn and how they might best learn it.

The use of artefacts as discussed here, aims to promote greater student engagement by empowering students in the selection and shaping of their work. It also encourages students to think creatively, in an often challenging study environment. The need for 'visioning' (Dunn *et al.* 2004), looking backwards and forwards, finding solutions to self-identified problems, draws upon and challenges this creative demand. Feedback after working with many of these artefacts is very positive. Although students are often apprehensive at first working in ways considered out of the ordinary, upon reflection they find the artefacts a valuable resource. The experience of artefact creation, and knowledge from this experience, can provide many unique and invaluable lessons.

We can see from Mark's case study that the artefacts embedded in the programme make it virtually impossible for the students to cheat or conduct any form of academic misconduct. This is accomplished through the individual and personal nature of the artefact development, regular formative feedback and the focus on self-reflection. More importantly, this case study demonstrates the power of authentic assessment on the development of students and their personal learning gain. The students develop fundamental, lifelong skills in their depth of understanding, self-awareness, critical thinking and in overcoming barriers to learning. The assessments outlined in the case study are engaging, empowering and promote active learning. They demonstrate the benefits of progressive learning and knowledge building, which are frequently missing in traditional 'snapshot' assessments such as essays and exams.

We previously discussed some of the common drivers for academic misconduct, but as evidenced by Mark's case study, the use of authentic assessments can overcome these.

- *Lack of time*: Assessment activities can be broken down into smaller tasks which build on learning throughout the study period, thus supporting the students in planning their time more effectively. Formative feedback throughout the process will further support the student and act as a motivator if planning and time management issues are evident.

- *Lack of subject knowledge*: The development of artefacts over a period of time will give students and academic staff the opportunity to identify knowledge gaps and further support learning. Tailored student support can be provided in directed study activities, furthering the development of skills to overcome personal and institutional barriers.

- *Lack of academic writing skills*: Authentic assessments provide more variety in the ways in which knowledge can be tested and this allows students to demonstrate their skills in multiple ways. For example, Case Study 12.2 demonstrates how digital skills are developed, and how cultural awareness skills are enhanced. Academic writing is still an essential skill required in education and support is necessary to advance growth in this area.

Key takeaways

As academics, we must recognise our role in promoting academic integrity through the development of assessments that are authentic, relevant and reflect the changing nature of the external environment. We must also reflect on our own academic practice as our role is far wider than designing assessments. Academics should role model the behaviours they expect to see in their students, thus avoiding many of the mistakes commonly made. For example, our teaching materials must be original or accurately cited and referenced; our assignments cannot remain unchanged from one cohort to another, we must use scholarly academic sources and we have to be consistent in our feedback to students.

Attempts to 'beat the cheats' will be a persistent battle; providers will continue to find ways of targeting students despite efforts to block or prevent their actions. Unfortunately, some students will continue to access contract cheating organisations and commit academic misconduct unless the key drivers are addressed and responded to. As academics, we must seek ways to address concerns surrounding academic integrity and the answer is not simple. However, we can recognise that our approach to learning, teaching and assessment design is integral to developing our students' knowledge, skills and overall attainment. Innovation and originality are fundamental to preparing our students for life after study. As we explored in Case Study 12.2, academics must be bold and seek out innovative ways of improving student learning through authentic assessment and experiences.

Inspired by this chapter? Why not try ...

- exploring the introduction of a US-style 'honour code' or student charter which outlines the responsibilities of students in maintaining academic integrity
- conducting a critical peer review of existing assessments to establish the likelihood of misconduct or contract cheating
- considering a programme-based approach to assessment which integrates assessment tasks across units/modules and focuses on a 'real-world' problem (see Hartley and Whitfield 2012)
- contacting local organisations and collaborating on immersive assessments
- inviting students to co-design their assessments so as to empower them and engage them in the assessment process

13 Embedding employability using innovation

TEF Principles this chapter refers to:

Student outcomes and learning gain: the extent to which all students achieve their educational and professional goals, in particular those from disadvantaged backgrounds

The use of the term 'employability' has become so widespread and overused that it has almost become a meaningless catch-all term. A useful point to start our discussion around embedding employability is to provide a little more focus by taking a couple of steps back and reflecting on two fundamental questions. First, where did the emphasis on employability come from? Second, what does it actually mean? Both these underlying questions are often obscured in the mass of work around 'employability' and yet are key to understanding what the issues actually are.

What does 'employability' mean and where did it come from?

So, where does the emphasis on employability as a key metric in post-compulsory education actually come from, particularly in relation to Higher Education? When did we move away from Newman's idea of the university as a place that teaches students 'to think and to reason and to discriminate and to analyse' (1852), to the view of universities as preparing, and being judged by how well they prepare, students for the graduate workplace? One answer to these questions lies in the increasingly widely held view amongst policy-makers over the last 30–40 years that advanced Western economies have come predominantly to be knowledge-based societies. Unlike the earlier industrial-based economies, which relied on physical capital accumulation, knowledge-based economies rely on the development of a society's stock of human resources (Becker 1964; Schultz 1971). This therefore puts the post-compulsory education sector, and Higher Education in particular, at the forefront of economic development.

In terms of post-compulsory education policy, regarding universities and colleges as drivers of economic growth has led to a shift in policy to what Shattock (2006) has referred to as an 'outside-in' approach. Policy-makers have increasingly taken a more coherent and centrally driven approach, underpinned by the view of universities and colleges as being the key to enhancing the stock of human resources to drive growth. This outside-in approach contrasts with the earlier Newmanesque inside-out view driven by the Haldane principle that, 'government funding of universities should be within institutional arrangements that ensured that it did not exert undue influence on what they did' (Haldane, cited in Boden and Nedeva 2010: 39). All the significant policy statements from the 1997 Dearing Report onwards reflect a more instrumental outside-in approach with measurable 'employability' metrics an increasingly key driver behind policy.

Moving to the second question of what does 'employability' actually mean, one of the most well-known definitions is that of Yorke (2004: 410), who describes it as:

"A set of achievements – skills, understandings and personal attributes – that make graduates more likely to gain employment and be successful in their chosen occupations, which benefit themselves, the workforce, the community and the economy"

Not only is this definition widely used in the literature around employability, but it also forms the basis, often with slight tweaks, of many institutional definitions around which internal employability strategies are built. Referring back to the discussion above, the link back to the notion of preparing students to be the drivers of the knowledge-based society are clearly evident.

However, when examined closely there are number of issues with this definition, particularly as a basis for embedding employability in the curriculum. In fact, the definition encapsulates one of the central problems that confuses the whole employability debate. If we accept it as *the* definition of employability, then we fail to recognise that there may in fact be two quite different perspectives of employability embodied within the definition. The statements 'likely to gain employment' and 'be successful in their chosen occupations' may actually be quite different perspectives on employability. The 'likely to gain employment' statement is an output-driven view, the student on completion of their course making a successful transition into the labour market, with 'successful' being determined by the sector metric. However, the 'be successful in their chosen career' statement represents a more open-ended view with employability seen as an ongoing developmental process which continues beyond one's studies in college or university. What is also important to recognise is that in some subject areas, the 'skills, understandings and personal attributes' required to make a successful transition into a chosen occupation may be quite different 'skills, understandings and personal attributes' than those required to develop a career within their chosen occupation.

The above discussion, and the reason for use of qualifiers such as 'may' in many of the comments, illustrates another weakness of trying to use a generic definition for 'employability'. Employability is both multidimensional and context specific. To illustrate, let us consider three cases.

Example 1: The Nursing student. For a student on a Nursing course, the distinction between the 'skills, understandings and personal attributes' needed to gain employment and to then subsequently develop a career in nursing are largely the same. Entry into the nursing profession is through completion of an accredited degree course that is based around the professional standards set nationally by the Nursing and Midwifery Council. The standards are highly prescriptive with significant practice and work-based experience as central requirements. We would perhaps be worried if that wasn't the case!

Example 2: A Business Management student. Many students on Business Management courses have aspirations of gaining a graduate training contract with a 'blue chip' company. For business management students, the 'skills, understandings and personal attributes' that would be developed through taking a Business degree would (hopefully) be of use in developing a career in business. However, unlike our nursing student, they are not sufficient in themselves to successfully gain a graduate training contract. To do this, our aspiring business student needs to understand how to play the labour market entry game. This will include constructing focused CVs, labour market search skills, understanding recruitment practices in different sectors, interview skills, maybe having to cope with an assessment centre or having a well-developed LinkedIn profile. This constitutes an entirely different skill set than those gained through their Business Management degree.

Example 3: A History student. It might be reasonable to expect that a History student might also aspire to gain a graduate training contract. However, for the History student the disjuncture between the skills and competencies developed on their course and those required to make a successful transition into a graduate training contract may be even greater than for the Business Management student.

The general point being made is that if we, as educators, are to address the employability agenda in a meaningful way to the benefit of our students, then we have to adopt a more nuanced approach to curriculum design than is usually reflected in institutional policy statements. Employability is an area where one size definitely does not fit all; indeed, as pointed out in our second case study later in the chapter, this might not even be the case at course level.

Employability as personal and professional development

Returning to Yorke's definition of employability, 'be successful in their chosen occupations' suggests a view of employability related to personal and professional development. As discussed previously, there is a strong subject context element to how the issue of embedding professional development is typically dealt with in curriculum design. For the Nursing student in example 1, professional and personal development are central to their course; however, this is less the case for our Business Management and History students. The focus is this section will be on these latter courses – those that are not driven by vocational professional competency standards.

For many of these non-professions linked courses, the most common approach has been to equate 'employability' with 'skills' and to build 'skills' modules within a course curriculum. The 'skills' module may go under a variety of titles but in many cases they reflect a similar set of 'generic skills' which are justified as being 'what the employer wants'. One typical list of generic skills can be found in the Confederation of British Industry report *Future fit: Preparing graduates for the world of work* (CBI 2009), which lists the following employability skills:

- Team working
- Business and customer awareness
- Problem-solving
- Communication and literacy
- Application of numeracy
- Application of information technology (although this one is increasingly being replaced by 'digital literacy')

It is not difficult to find endless examples of variations on this list of 'soft skills' from a range of sources.

The essentially bolt-on nature of this type of skills module, even where they try to hide behind titles such as 'Professional Skills for X', leads, in many cases, to poor student engagement, poor feedback and poor module evaluations. Students simply do not see the point of these 'soft skills' within the context of their course – they are motivated by learning about engineering/accountancy/biology, not how to do a presentation or work in a team. Holmes (2013) refers to this sort of approach to employability as the 'possessional' approach, with graduate employability being seen as developing skills and attributes '... as if they are capable of being processed and used' (Holmes 2013: 540). This is a very passive view of employability – students are having things done to them to because we (the educators) think it will make them more employable.

Our first case study by Susan Smith presents an example of how, by embedding professionally relevant skills within a subject module, and using them as central to an authentic assessment, many of the pitfalls of bolt-on skills modules can be avoided.

Case study 13.1: Bridging the gap between graduate skills and those valued by employers

Susan Smith, University of Sussex

This case sought to address the reported gap between graduates' skills and those most valued by employers (Jackling and De Lange 2009; Howcroft

2017). The literature evidences the challenge faced by educators to find a balance between developing technical and generic skills and suggests that authentic assessment (Ashford-Rowe *et al.* 2014) can help to address the apparent gap without resulting in a loss of technical skill.

The module involved was a final-year undergraduate option in auditing. The module typically attracts around 50 students and the coursework assessment was a group case study, which culminated in a report. To develop the generic skills as an embedded part of the curriculum and authentic experience, the lecturers incorporated a mini audit into the coursework as an optional alternative to the case study after trialling it with students as a voluntary exercise in the first year. Students work in groups on the coursework, since audit is a group activity, and thus the ability to form a productive group and work effectively as a group member is important.

This involved students being set a discrete controls area to audit by the client and producing a report and suitable recommendations. Over the last three academic years, two teams have taken advantage of this opportunity each year. In each year, a different experience was arranged with local businesses. The client interaction has typically taken the form of a client meeting with senior management and others within the organisation at the client site, combined with the opportunity for up to three follow-up emails. The client was asked to provide feedback on a number of areas including professionalism, group work, communication skills and the report (Jones 2014).

After the first cycle, we included a reflective element into the assessment to enable students to differentiate themselves and to prompt thought around their skills development. This provided some useful feedback on the experience, which is difficult to capture by other means because not all students on the module undertook the experience. It also offered insight into why some students selected this opportunity and others did not. It was informative to learn that some students did not select the experience, as they were fearful that it would be harder than the case study despite acknowledging that it was a good opportunity. Those who did undertake it cited a need to build their experiences and the excitement of the opportunity.

"After considering the audit experience I realised it was a rare chance which would be very beneficial to my curriculum vitae"

(Student)

The challenge for this type of experience is to find a way to scale it to ensure that it can become the default coursework rather than offered as an option. In addition, it has been found that it is important to fully brief the students on business etiquette for meetings (e.g. to introduce oneself, make notes, have an agenda and clear lines of questioning), as they do not know what to expect and often feel anxious about talking to the client. For example, one team forgot to introduce themselves, and another hadn't planned who would ask which questions before the visit.

The primary outcome has been the development of the students' generic skills. It is clear from the reflective writing that the students who have undertaken the experience have a greater understanding of the importance of working together effectively and of presenting a cohesive approach to the client. Their reflections self-identified similar strengths and weaknesses as the client. In addition, the students had some understanding of how to apply the audit skills they had learned in a real-life situation. Those who had undertaken this opportunity were noticeably more engaged for the remainder of the module. The primary limitation is the scale of the experience and the barriers to offering it to all students on the module. This might be achieved by reconstituting the client experience. For example, the client could present the challenge to the whole class, then groups could interview various client staff in rotation for a short period of time to gather additional insight.

Susan's case study demonstrates an alternative approach to the bolt-on skills module to recognise that professional development, whether based around generic skills development or some wider set of competencies, goes hand-in-hand with personal development. In turn, this implies that 'skills development' is something that is unique to each individual student, and recognises not only the subject context but the student's disposition, background experiences and future aspirations. More importantly, this view reflects a different more student-centric strand within the employability literature where the employability element of a course is based around the need for the students to develop their own graduate identity. From this perspective, a student's employability is not developed through just passively acquiring employability skills but by students actively engaging with their own personal development needs. Hinchcliffe and Jolly (2011) argue that course teams should not focus just on developing skills in a passive manner but on providing students with 'graduate experiences'. The graduate experiences, complemented by employability skills, will enable a student to develop a personal capability set which forms the basis of their unique graduate identity (Hinchcliffe and Jolly 2011; Stevenson and Clegg 2011; Holmes 2013, 2015). Holmes (2013: 548) refers to this more student-centric, active view of employability as a 'positional' approach: '… individuals make a difference … by *what they do*, the actions they take'.

Essentially, what we are saying is that students need to be given some control over the development of their professional skills. This does not mean that generic skills, such as those in the CBI list, are not important, simply that students need to recognise their relevance for themselves. Students need to realise, for example, that to be able to give a short presentation will be important for them in the future, a skill that at the moment they do not possess. The course curriculum needs to be designed to give students the opportunity to develop their own graduate identity. In our second case study, Mary Crossan outlines an ambitious approach taken within a Business School to give a degree of control to students to recognise their development needs and act upon those perceived needs.

Case study 13.2: A CPD approach to developing student employability

Mary Crossan, Coventry University

Over the last five years, student rep feedback forums have increasingly highlighted the concerns around skills-based modules and how, when considering employability, one size does not fit all. The School of Strategy and Leadership within Coventry Business School decided to explore this issue further and see what pedagogical innovations could address employability within the course and curriculum.

The course team took the feedback from students, together with what employers from industry were wanting from their graduates, and developed an innovative suite of CPD (Continuous Professional Development) modules. This employability initiative was added to all our undergraduate Business courses, allowing students to self-select and drive their employability journey within the curriculum. It was placed in all three levels of study from Year 1 through to final-year students, which was on average 500 students per year, over 1500 students at any one time. The aims were to mirror CPD that takes place within the world of work, allowing students to experience self-development, and encourage a reflective approach, before being required to do so within their career.

"You really appreciate the CPD modules when you are in employment and look back at what those modules were trying to achieve. I have a real focus on CPD and improving myself and I think some of this is thanks to the CPD modules I had during my UG degree in Business Management. We all should be looking for the next course or activity to increase our opportunity for learning and gaining knowledge"

(BA Business Management alumni)

The CPD modules also aimed to support students in developing the skills they will need to compete in the graduate labour market after graduation.

The CPD suite of modules has undergone a number of pilots and changes since its inception in 2015 but the aims remain the same. Initially, there were a mix of mandatory sessions and optional choices, that worked for some students but not for all. The modules were then moved to a completely free choice approach, which worked well for engaged and focused students, but meant that the less engaged students struggled, as they could not pass the assessment if they had not collected points by signing up and attending CPD sessions which awarded them points. One major issue students had was managing their time for the CPD sessions. As this was a bespoke pick-and-mix approach, the support systems also struggled in parts, particularly in relation to timetabling. CPD sessions didn't appear on timetables and students forgot what they signed up for and had to attend. This was envisaged by the development team and seen as part of the learning experience, managing themselves – something which students could and should reflect on within their assessment.

Assessment was based on students gaining CPD points through attending sessions and undertaking a range of activities. A reflective journal of their CPD activities and personal learning and development was the basis of their coursework assignment. However, in order to complete the reflective journal, students had to have attended sufficient sessions and workshops to gain the points. An inability to secure the necessary points resulted in an automatic fail. The final portfolio was assessed on a pass/fail basis.

The course team feel that the traditional employability skills module sought to equip students, usually in their final year, with information and some practical support to help them navigate the traditional milk-round style approach to graduate recruitment that remains typical in the UK. However, with an increasing proportion of students coming from overseas, many of whom intend to work in the family business, and more students seeking non-traditional forms of employment after graduation, the employability module has become less relevant and appropriate. Even for those home students looking for more traditional routes into the graduate labour market, a generic employability skills module would fail to cater to the range of needs found within the group. This may typically range from a student who has been out on a full-year work placement and has already guaranteed post-graduation employment, to a student who has not even thought about what they are going to do post-graduation.

Instead, our CPD modules offer students a hybrid approach. For those students at the very start of their employability journey, there is the option to follow a structured programme of practical workshops which will build their skills over the three years of their undergraduate degree to make sure they have the basics, such as a CV. Students who are more advanced in their career planning can create their own bespoke programmes of employability-related activities, from seminars on self-employment to the Institute of Directors mentoring scheme. Students report that they welcome this balance between structure and flexibility and this approach allows the modules to evolve as we respond to feedback from students themselves and employers.

To date, the results have been mixed between students who love the CPD modules and the personal development they can gain, and students who want to tick the box by submitting an assignment to pass this stage of study. In theory, the CPD suite of modules are an excellent idea and a welcome addition to the UG Business courses, although in reality the administration and time taken to run such modules is considerable and should not be underestimated. However, the applied and practical approach to the CPD suite of modules we see as being key to readying our students for the world of work, also keeps courses current and relevant to what is happening in the world of work. Ultimately, the CPD suite of modules prepares our students for life as well as graduation and beyond. That is the real purpose of why we as academics run such modules, isn't it?

It is true to say that the pass rates on this module took a dip when implementing the CPD suite of modules, as there was a move to making engagement and taking part in activities a requirement of passing the module; late or unengaged students therefore struggled in a way they didn't with other modules.

However, the value impact for the CPD modules is less about scores and statistics and more about the value perceived by students in directing them in the right directions upon graduation. There is evidence of more favourable feedback on these modules in Student Rep feedback meetings and increased student engagement with elements outside the course delivery.

There is a tension between giving a positive student experience which helps support and develop the individual student journey and enhancement of their transferable skills ready for graduation and progression into the world of work or further study.

One of the many interesting features of Mary's case study is the recognition by the course team of the distinction between employability as self-development and employability as gaining that first graduate job. As discussed earlier for students graduating from profession-linked courses which are closely defined by professional standards and include significant elements of work-based learning, progression into the profession is relatively clear-cut. The nature of course they have taken is largely driven by the need for students to develop their individual personal capabilities and a graduate identity reflecting their chosen profession. This is often further strengthened by professional body accreditation confirming a student's graduate identity.

For our Business Management or History graduate who wishes to land a Graduate Training Contract with a blue-chip company, the 'likely to gain employment' part of the Yorke employability definition is not quite as clear-cut. Even if they have taken advantage of the opportunities offered through their course for personal development and developing their own distinct graduate identity, this is not by itself going to land the elusive training contract. It may be an obvious point to make but the single most important factor for a university graduate remains the class of degree they achieve – students who get first class degrees are more likely to gain graduate level jobs straight after graduation (Smetherham 2006; Mason *et al.* 2009). The other less tangible, but intuitively obvious factor, relates to a student's personal and demographic background and their related accumulated social capital (supported by evidence from a large-scale study undertaken in the early 2000s: Blasko *et al.* 2002; Brennan and Shah 2003). More recent evidence suggests that another important impact factor is relevant work experience, which may play an important role in developing a graduate identity for those students with less social capital (Holmes 2015; Cashian 2016).

However, even though a first class degree and the right social connections significantly enhance our aspiring Business Management or History graduate's chances of gaining a blue-chip training contract, it by no means guarantees it. The student still needs to develop the skills associated with playing the graduate labour market entry game, which will vary by sector and nature of the job. The key point though is that the market entry skills may not be the same as the CBI list of soft skills referred to earlier. Writing a focused CV, being prepared for an assessment centre, developing a LinkedIn profile, having a strong (and appropriate!) social media profile are all possible 'skills' that a student may need to make a successful transition into their chosen graduate career.

Key takeaways

The main focus of this chapter has been the need for a more nuanced approach at the curriculum design stage, if courses are to truly address the employability of their students. In those subject areas where there is no direct, externally defined link between the course and the subsequent career, then curriculum design needs to avoid the conflation of developmental employability ('be successful in their chosen career') and getting the first graduate job ('likely to gain employment'). The two employability perspectives may be built around two complementary but differing skill sets. The other key focus has been the need for students to be actively engaged in developing their own employability, not (unengaged) passive receivers of pre-determined 'employability skills'. The two case studies in this chapter offer good examples of innovative practice to address these issues. Both offer pointers to how the employability element of a course can be engaging, relevant and actually helpful to students and, in Yorke's terms, hopefully 'benefit themselves, the workforce, the community and the economy' (2004: 410).

In summary, it is important to recognise:

- the multifaceted and context-dependent nature of employability
- the need to be clear between employability as personal and professional development and employability as preparation for making a successful transition into the graduate labour market
- that curriculum design needs to focus on motivating students to actively engage in developing their own employability

---

Inspired by this chapter? Why not try ...

- *involving your careers support staff and employers in designing a student-centric employability input to your module*
- *inviting recent alumni to work with your students, particularly first-in-family students to raise their post-graduation aspirations*

14 Conclusion

TEF Principles this chapter refers to:

Teaching quality: teaching that stimulates and challenges students, and maximises engagement with their studies

Learning environment: resources and activities to support learning and improve retention, progression and attainment

Student outcomes and learning gain: the extent to which all students achieve their educational and professional goals, in particular those from disadvantaged background

So, as we draw towards the end of this book, it has become clear that there are three interconnected themes that need to be addressed, challenged and planned for if colleges and universities can truly claim to be innovative and ready to meet the challenges of the future. The exact responses to these themes are likely to be establishment specific – indeed, another theme that we might have included is that increasingly a 'one size fits all' approach is not always appropriate – but an understanding of each theme will go a long way towards establishing a strategy that will help develop the goals of the organisation.

Performativity and commercialisation

The point has been made on a number of occasions in this book that performativity and commercialisation should not always be looked at in purely *negative* terms. Simmons' (2008) work on the impact of incorporation on colleges makes this point clearly. Whilst the environment that existed prior to the 1992 Further and Higher Education Act is often viewed as a golden age, Simmons identifies the lack of efficiency, waste of resources and lack of consideration of the needs of the students as reasons why this seminal Act should not always be looked upon in purely negative terms.

Performativity and commercialisation have given rise to a large number of measures of performance and whilst there is sometimes a degree of cynicism about metrics, captured well by Orr (2012: 58) who talks about how the sector now has the 'ability to speak fluently the language of performativity', it is certainly true that there is now considerably more information available for students to consider when making an informed choice of which establishment to go to. This wealth of information, however, can be overwhelming and there is an inbuilt assumption that students have the knowledge and understanding to be able to make such informed choices. Both colleges and universities have become adept at selecting the metrics that best suit their marketing needs and whilst that can be a positive from a competitive advantage point of view, it does not necessarily facilitate students to make the right choice for themselves.

This increased amount of information on offer to students is further complicated by their changing role. Students have become active stakeholders rather than passive recipients of education. The benefit of this can be seen in the significant increase in focus on the needs of students. *Student experience* is something that is viewed as sacrosanct in both colleges and universities and the measures that identify the best providers in this area, such as the TEF and the NSS, are key indicators for all organisations.

Whilst this increased focus on the needs of the student can be viewed in a positive light, the negative side of increased commercialisation can be seen in the change in the perceived role of students – as customers or consumers (Tomlinson 2017): the competition engendered in the sector means that institutions have become service providers, focused on securing the student for the institution rather than what is best for the individual.

This reframing of the relationship between institution, performance and student has been a key feature of education post-92 and with the advent of the REF, TEF, QAA and Ofsted inspections, there is a growing danger for institutions. Practices such as benchmarking against best practice are common and there is a growing realisation that professionalism amongst institutional management is of vital importance. All of this has created a sector that feels far more regimented than before and indeed, far more homogeneous. Each institution searches out best practice and adopts it for themselves, albeit with minor alterations.

Whilst this increased professionalism should not be viewed in a wholly negative light, it does create risks. By seeking out best practice the danger is that innovation and alternative solutions will be stifled as organisations search out 'safe' solutions. When metrics determine not only reputation but in some cases the funding of the organisation, a risk-averse culture becomes prevalent. At a time when the student base has become more diversified than ever before, this can be seen as a major problem. We have stressed at regular stages that a 'one size fits all' approach does not work within education. A university with a strong widening participation remit will need to have a very different approach to a Russell Group establishment, yet the measurements used encourage this push towards homogeneity as the criteria for each metric are clearly defined. Counterintuitively, we have seen that individuals who do not follow a common trend and take an alternative path tend to succeed. They do this by focusing on what they perceive as being excellent and frame it with reference to the student experience. If the student is happy, the experience positive and the approach results in more motivated staff and students, the metrics tend to take care of themselves. This approach reverses the normal view that you look at the metrics and work out how to get the best possible result. By focusing on the process, rather than the end result, you can explore new and innovative approaches which allow for a diversified student base and also encourage staff to explore new solutions. This leads to more empowered workforce as well as a culture whereby targets are met without the need to focus entirely on them.

Towards different teaching approaches

It is easy to see the COVID-19 pandemic in isolation and to hypothesise that it will be a sudden catalyst for change, but this would be a rather more simplistic supposition than the evidence suggests. The truth is that there has been a defined movement away from traditional pedagogy for some time now and whilst the pandemic might have hastened things along and altered many perceptions about what is meant by teaching in Further and Higher Education, COVID-19 is a mere stepping-stone on the path to a change in the relationship between lecturer and student.

When the University of Northampton opened its new Waterfront Campus in 2018, it was hailed as a further step towards a new approach to learning. A key feature was that all accommodation was flexible and so it was possible to move away from lectures and seminars to approaches that were more innovative and potentially better suited to learners' needs. Whilst having a brand new campus is undoubtedly of benefit when planning new approaches, older buildings are not necessarily an insurmountable obstacle to innovation in the curriculum. The use of digital learning has been a key feature during the recent pandemic and is undoubtedly something that many organisations will be keen to continue in the future, but there are other innovations that can also help redefine how teaching is perceived.

The assumption in Further and Higher Education is that students are actively involved in the learning process and should be co-creators of the lesson. This approach, which borrows much from the theory of andragogy espoused by Knowles (1984), is both aspirational and flawed. Ensuring that students are active, engaged learners is comparatively easy among mature students but the assumption that these techniques can be transferred to younger students, without preparing them in any way, is not one that can be embraced. Whilst organisations often talk about student engagement, the truth is that this is not something that can just occur, it needs to be planned for and all stakeholders need to be involved.

Some organisations have tried to address this by changing their induction procedures, by increasing student representation at all levels of the organisation and by encouraging innovation amongst staff, but there are still many obstacles to overcome. The danger of merely benchmarking against competitors has been covered elsewhere and a change in culture is needed, but there are even more fundamental barriers that need to be looked at. Traditionally within Higher Education, a mixture of lectures and seminars has been used and whilst it is possible to innovate and engage in seminars, lectures, which might be attended by several hundred students, are more difficult to innovate.

Many alternative approaches have been used – flipped classrooms, pre-reading and digital engagement have become common features in both Further and Higher Education – but they depend on a collaborative approach between student and lecturer. Given the diverse nature of both students and indeed lecturers in education, this can be a challenge. Ensuring students are well prepared for their studies and that they engage with materials is something that needs to be done from the start, but lecturers need to engage also. The University of Maastricht is one institution that has taken an innovative approach to this. Every seminar revolves around problem-based learning, with students expected to solve a problem rather than merely being passive receptors of knowledge. This not only encourages students to explore new areas but also staff are given the freedom and direction to engage in these techniques. Without clear direction from the organisation, the likelihood is that most students and staff would lapse into techniques that they had used previously.

To cope with the diversity of learners and the importance of learning being a collaborative activity, many organisations talk about personalisation whereby students control their own learning. Whilst there are challenges to this, which may range from resource implications to financial challenges, the main problem often lies with preparation of students (and staff) for this way of working. Meeting each individual need in a lecture of over 200 is not possible but if students work collaboratively and take control of their own learning, then this is more achievable.

At the heart of this control is the assessment regime. Students often see assessment as a barrier to be overcome after learning has taken place rather than an integral part of the learning process. The change that is needed is to switch the emphasis on assessment, and indeed the whole learning process, from an instrumental approach, underpinned by metrics, regular hurdles to be cleared and a one-way communication process from lecturer down to student, to one that is far more collaborative.

There are multiple techniques that can be used to facilitate this. The integration of assessment in the form of authentic and personalised assessments is a good start but also the importance of preparing both students and staff cannot be underestimated. Technology is an underlying enabler to the achievement of this aim, but it is not the whole answer. To enable different approaches, there needs to be expectations from the start and clear communication to all parties. There also needs to be a change in culture and clear directives from the organisation – moving to a new building can certainly help this process but the University of Maastricht and others have shown that by changing the culture, and putting in place a clear objective, it is possible to redefine your teaching approach and change the student-lecturer relationship.

The changing nature of a practitioner's professional identity

Our final thread ties together the previous two points made and focuses on the academic as an individual and how their own professional identity has changed and will change further. The shift in emphasis from 'teaching' to 'learning' has been a notable feature of the last twenty years. Ofsted stresses the lesson as a whole, rather than focus on the individual teacher and that is a practice that has permeated through the sector.

When asked why they chose teaching, many new entrants will focus on the importance of giving something back. Inherent in this statement is a feeling that the lecturer has knowledge that they are looking to pass on to others. This 'sage on the stage' approach mirrors the traditional lecturing approach where interaction is minimal and the focus is very much on the person at the front. The shift to the 'guide at the side' requires a different mindset and the alternative teaching strategies discussed previously. This change is a challenge for many lecturers, as there are worries about loss of control as well as the difficulty in seeing students as co-learners not empty vessels to be filled.

What this means is that a lecturer in education today needs to develop a professional identity which goes beyond subject expertise to include professional practice around supporting collaborative subject learning. This can be a challenge and means that inductions for organisations need to be looked at and refocused to ensure that subject experts are also aware of the wider issues within education. Organisations also need to stress the importance of professional development that is focused on supporting the development of professional practice rather than merely subject pedagogy. This wider approach, whilst more difficult to formalise and codify, is of vital importance if innovative approaches are to be introduced. Strong subject knowledge is of course important for any academic but having the confidence to go beyond that to try new approaches is of vital importance in making sure that academics are able to put in place the innovative approaches that will ensure the continuing success of the organisation and wider education landscape.

References

Ade-Ojo, G. and Duckworth, V. (2015) *Adult Literacy Policy and Practice: From Intrinsic Values to Instrumentalism*. Basingstoke: Palgrave Macmillan.

Advance HE (2019) *Internationalising higher education*. Available from <https://www.advance-he.ac.uk/guidance/teaching-and-learning/internationalisation>

Akinbosede, D. (2019) *The BAME attainment gap is not the fault of BAME students* [online]. Available from <https://www.timeshighereducation.com/opinion/bame-attainment-gap-not-fault-bame-students>

Ali, N., Ahmed, L. and Rose, S. (2017) 'Identifying predictors of students' perception and engagement with assessment feedback'. *Active Learning in Higher Education* 19 (3): 239–251.

Alsup, J. (2006) *Teacher Identity Discourses: Negotiating Personal and Professional Spaces*. New York: Routledge.

Amigud, A. and Dawson, P. (2020) 'The law and the outlaw: Is legal prohibition a viable solution to the contract cheating problem?' *Assessment & Evaluation in Higher Education* 45 (1): 98–108.

Anderson, L.W. and Burns, R.B. (1989) *Research in Classrooms: The Study of Teachers, Teaching and Instruction*. Oxford: Pergamon Press.

Anderson, R. (2016) *University fees in historical perspective*. History & Policy. Available from <https://www.historyandpolicy.org/policy-papers/papers/univeristy-fees-in-historical-perspective>

Arnab, S., Clarke, S. and Morini, M. (2019a) 'Co-creativity through play and game design thinking'. *Electronic Journal of E-Learning* 17 (3): 184–198.

Arnab, S., Jacey, L., Fitri, M., Morini, L. and Clarke, S. (2019b) 'Creativeculture: Can teachers be game designers?' In *Proceedings of the 13th International Conference on Game Based Learning, ECGBL 2019*, 32–40.

Ashford-Rowe, K., Herrington, J. and Brown, C. (2014) 'Establishing the critical elements that determine authentic assessment'. *Assessment and Evaluation in Higher Education* 39 (2): 205–222.

Atkinson, P.A. (2013) 'Blowing hot: The ethnography of craft and the craft of ethnography'. *Qualitative Inquiry* 19 (5): 397–404.

Ball, S. (2003) 'The teacher's soul and the terrors of performativity'. *Journal of Education Policy* 18 (2): 215–228.

Barber, M., Donnelly, K. and Rizvi, S. (2013) *An avalanche is coming: Higher education and the revolution ahead*. Available from <https://www.ippr.org/files/images/media/files/publication/2013/04/avalanche-is-coming_Mar2013_10432.pdf>

Barkas, L., Scott, J., Poppitt, N. and Smith, P. (2017) 'Tinker, tailor, policy-maker: Can the UK government's teaching excellence framework deliver its objectives?' *Journal of Further and Higher Education* 43 (6): 801–813.

Bates, E.A. and Kaye, L.K. (2014) '"I'd be expecting caviar in lectures": The impact of the new fee regime on undergraduate students' expectations of Higher Education'. *Higher Education* 67 (5): 655–673.

Becker, G.S. (1964) *Human Capital*. Chicago, IL: Chicago University Press.

Beetham, H., McGill, L. and Littlejohn, A. (2009) *Thriving in the 21st century: Learning Literacies for the Digital Age (LLiDA project)*. UK Joint Information Systems Committee (JISC).

Behets, D. (1993) 'Systematic observation training for preservice physical education teachers'. *Physical Educator* 50 (2): 87–94.

Bell, A. and Santamaria, L.J. (2018) *Understanding Experiences of First Generation University Students: Culturally Responsive and Sustaining Methodologies.* London: Bloomsbury.

Bell, R., Barrett, K. and Allison, P. (1985) 'What preservice physical education teachers see in an unguided, early field experience'. *Journal of Teaching in Physical Education* 4 (2): 81–90.

Berger, P. and Luckmann, T. (1966) *The Social Construction of Reality.* London: Penguin Books.

Beynon, H. (1975) *Working for Ford.* Wakefield: EP Publishing.

Biggs, J. and Tang, C. (2011) *Teaching for Quality Learning at University*, 4th edition. Maidenhead: Open University Press.

Binns, C. (2019) *Experiences of Academics from a Working-Class Heritage: Ghosts of Childhood Habitus.* Cambridge: Cambridge Scholars Publishing.

Blasko, Z., Brennan, J., Little, B. and Shah, T. (2002) *Access to what? Analysis of the factors determining graduate employability.* A report to the HEFCE by the Centre for Education Research and Information (CHERI). Available from <https://dera.ioe.ac.uk/5366/1/rd14_02a.pdf>

Bloomfield, D., Taylor, N. and Maxwell, D. (2004) 'Enhancing the link between university and schools through action research on teaching practicum'. *Journal of Vocational Education and Training* 56 (3): 355–372.

Boden, R. and Nedeva, M. (2010) 'Employing discourse: Universities and graduate employability'. *Journal of Education Policy* 25 (1): 37–54.

Bonwell, C.C. and Eison, J.A. (1991) *Active Learning: Creating Excitement in the Classroom.* ASHE-ERIC Higher Education Report No. 1. Washington, DC: The George Washington University, School of Education and Human Development.

Brennan, J. and Shah, T. (2003) *Access to what? Converting educational opportunity into employment opportunity.* Final report. London: Centre for Education Research and Information (CHERI).

Bretag, T. (2018) *Academic integrity.* Available from <https://oxfordre.com/business/view/10.1093/acrefore/9780190224851.001.0001/acrefore-9780190224851-e-147#acrefore-9780190224851-e-147-bibItem-0128>

Bretag, T., Harper, R., Burton, M., Ellis, C., Newton, P., Rozenberg, P. *et al.* (2019) 'Contract cheating: A survey of Australian university students'. *Studies in Higher Education* 44 (11): 1837–1856.

Brimble, M. and Stevenson-Clarke, P. (2005) 'Perceptions of the prevalence and seriousness of academic dishonesty in Australian universities'. *Australian Educational Researcher* 32 (3): 19–44.

Britzman, D. (2003) *Practice Makes Practice.* New York: SUNY Press.

Brown, C. and Czerniewicz, L. (2010) 'Debunking the "digital native": Beyond digital apartheid, towards digital democracy'. *Journal of Computer Assisted Learning* 26 (5): 357–369.

Brown, S. (2004) 'Assessment for learning'. *Learning and Teaching in Higher Education* 1: 2004–05.

Brown, S. (2013) 'Internationalising assessment, learning and teaching'. *AISHE-J: The All Ireland Journal of Teaching and Learning in Higher Education* 5 (2): 1311–1317.

Bruner, J.S. (1961) 'The act of discovery'. *Harvard Educational Review* 31 (1): 21–32.

Bunce, L., Baird, A. and Jones, S. (2017) 'The student as consumer approach in Higher Education and its effects on academic performance'. *Studies in Higher Education* 42 (11): 1958–1978.

Callaghan, J. (1976) *A rational debate based on the facts.* Available from <http://www.educationengland.org.uk/documents/speeches/1976ruskin.html>

Cashian, P.S. (2016) 'Developing a more coherent and robust basis for employability research: A critical realist perspective'. In Tomlinson, M. and Holmes, L., eds., *Graduate Employability in Context: Research, Theory and Debate.* London: Palgrave Macmillan.

Caughlan, S. and Heng, J. (2014) 'Observation and teacher quality: Critical analysis of observational instruments in preservice teacher performance assessment'. *Journal of Teacher Education* 65 (5): 375–388.

Clarke, R. and Lancaster, T. (2006) 'Eliminating the successor to plagiarism? Identifying the usage of contract cheating sites'. In *Proceedings of 2nd Plagiarism: Prevention, Practice and Policy Conference 2006,* Newcastle, UK.

Coe, R. (2014) *Classroom observation: It's harder than you think.* Available from <https://www.cem.org/blog/414/>

Coffield, F. (2017) *Will the Leopard Change its Spots? A New Model of Inspection for Ofsted.* London: Institution of Education.

Coffield, F. and Williamson, B. (2011) *From Exam Factories to Communities of Discovery: The Democratic Route.* London: Institute of Education.

Coldron, J. and Smith, R. (1999) 'Active location in teachers' construction of their professional identities'. *Journal of Curriculum Studies* (31) 6, 711–726.

Confederation of British Industry (CBI) (2009) *Future fit: Preparing graduates for the world of work.* Available from <https://www.universitiesuk.ac.uk/policy-and-analysis/reports/Documents/2009/future-fit-preparing-graduates-for-the-world-of-work.PDF>

Connolly, B. (2009) *Algebra.* Available from <https://www.youtube.com/watch?v=−JqZo07Ot-uA>

Cova, B. and Dalli, D. (2009) 'Working consumers: The next step in marketing theory?' *Marketing Theory* 9 (3): 315–339.

Croll, P. (1986) *Systematic Classroom Observation.* Lewes: Falmer Press.

Davis, J. and Fantozzi, V. (2016) 'What do student teachers want in mentor teachers? Desired, expected, possible, and emerging roles'. *Mentoring and Tutoring: Partnership in Learning* 24 (3): 250–266.

Dearing, R. (1997) *Higher Education in the Learning Society: Report of the National Committee of Inquiry into Higher Education* (The Dearing Report). London: HMSO. Available from <http://www.educationengland.org.uk/documents/dearing1997/dearing1997.html>

Dearlove, J. (1995) 'Collegiality, managerialism and leadership in English universities'. *Tertiary Education and Management* 1 (2): 161–169.

de Main, L. (2017) *Being voiceless: Perceptions of class, identity, misrepresentation and disconnect from a working class perspective.* Unpublished thesis. Coventry: Coventry University.

de Neve, K. and Heppner, M. (1997) 'Role play simulations: The assessment of an active learning technique and comparisons with traditional lectures'. *Innovative Higher Education* 21 (3): 231–246.

Department for Education (DfE) (1992) *Further and Higher Education Act.* London: HMSO.

Department for Education (DfE) (2019) *Widening participation in higher education, England, 2017/18 age cohort – Official statistics.* London: DfE. Available from <https://assets.publishing.service.gov.uk/government/uploads/system/uploads/attachment_data/file/852633/WP2019-MainText.pdf>

de Waal, K. and Fremantle, E. (2016) *The Mechanics' Institute Review Issue 13: New Stories from Birkbeck.* London: Birkbeck.

Dewey, J. (1933) *How We Think: A Restatement of the Relation of Reflective Thinking to the Education Process*. New York: D.C. Heath.

Didau, D. (2018) *Modelling and observation: A low threat model for teacher development*. Available from <https://learningspy.co.uk/training/modelling-and-observation>

Donne, J. (1624) 'Mediation XVII'. In *Devotions upon Emergent Occasions and Several Steps in my Sickness*. London: Printed by A.M. for Thomas Jones. Available from <https://www.gutenberg.org/files/23772/23772-h/23772-h.htm>

Draper, M.J. and Newton, P. (2017) 'A legal approach to tackling contract cheating'. *International Journal for Educational Integrity* 13 (11). Available from <https://link.springer.com/article/10.1007/s40979-017-0022-5>

Dudley, P. (2010) *Lesson study: A handbook*. Available from <http://lessonstudy.co.uk/wp-content/uploads/2012/03/new-handbook-revisedMay14.pdf>

Dunn, L., Morgan, C., O'Reilly, M. and Parry, S. (2004) *The Student Assessment Handbook: New Directions in Tradition and Online Assessment*. Abingdon: Routledge.

Ellis, C., van Haeringen, K., Harper, R., Bretag, T., Zucker, I., McBride, S. *et al.* (2020) 'Does authentic assessment assure academic integrity? Evidence from contract cheating data'. *Higher Education Research and Development* 39 (3): 454–469.

Ellis, K. and Johnston, C. (2019) *Pathways to university from care: Findings report one*. Sheffield: University of Sheffield. Available from <https://figshare.shef.ac.uk/articles/Pathways_to_University_from_Care_Recommendations_for_Universities/9578930>

Else, H. (2017) *To me, contextualised admissions policies smack of double standards and snobbery*. Available from <https://www.timeshighereducation.com/blog/me-contextualised-admissions-policies-smack-double-standards-and-snobbery>

Environmental Association for Universities and Colleges (EAUC) (2020) *Green Gown Awards*. Available from <https://www.greengownawards.org/home>

Ertmer, P. and Newby, T. (2013) 'Behaviourism, cognitivism, constructivism: Comparing critical features from an instructional design perspective'. *Performance Improvement Quarterly* 26 (2): 43–71.

Feiman-Nemser, S. (1998) 'Teachers as teacher educators'. *European Journal of Teacher Education* 21 (1): 63–74.

Fielden, J. (2011) *Getting to Grips with Internationalisation: Resources for UK Higher Education Institutions*. London: Leadership Foundation for Higher Education.

Fish, D. (1995) *Quality Mentoring for Student Teachers: A Principled Approach to Practice*. London: David Fulton.

Foucault, M. (1980) *Power/Knowledge: Selected Interviews and Other Writings 1972–1977*. Hassocks: Harvester Press.

Freebody, P. (2003) *Qualitative Research in Education: Interaction and Practice*. London: Sage.

Freire, P. (1970) *Pedagogy of the Oppressed*. New York: Herder & Herder.

Glendinning, I. (2014) 'Responses to student plagiarism in higher education across Europe'. *International Journal for Educational Integrity* 10 (1): 4–20.

Goffman, I. (1956) *The Presentation of Self in Everyday Life*. New York: Vintage Books.

Göktürk, E. (2005) *What is 'paradigm'?* Available from <http://citeseerx.ist.psu.edu/viewdoc/download?doi=10.1.1.697.4205&rep=rep1&type=pdf>

Gould, J. (2012) *Learning Theory and Classroom Practice in the Lifelong Learning Sector*. 2nd edition. London: Learning Matters.

Green, A. (1995) 'Technical education and state formation in nineteenth-century England and France'. *History of Education* 24 (2): 123–139.

Guilbault, M. (2016) 'Students as customers in higher education: Reframing the debate'. *Journal of Marketing for Higher Education* 26 (2): 132–142.

Guilford, J.P. (1967) *The Nature of Human Intelligence*. New York: McGraw-Hill.

Haggar, H., Burn, K. and McIntyre, D. (1993) *The School Mentor Handbook*. London: Kogan Page.

Hamza, M.K. and Griffith, K.G. (2006) 'Fostering problem solving and creative thinking in the classroom: Cultivating a creative mind.' *National Forum of Applied Educational Research Journal* 19 (3): 1–15.

Hartley, P. and Whitfield, R. (2012) *Programme Assessment Strategies (PASS)*. York: Higher Education Academy. Available from <https://www.bradford.ac.uk/pass/about/PASS_final_report.pdf>

Hascher, T., Cocard, Y. and Moser, P. (2004) 'Forget about theory – practice is all? Student teachers' learning in practicum'. *Teachers and Teaching* 10 (6): 623–637.

Heffernan, T., Morrison, D., Magne, P., Payne, S. and Cotton, D. (2019) 'Internalising internationalisation: Views of internationalisation of the curriculum among non-mobile home students'. *Studies in Higher Education* 44 (12): 2359–2373.

Hendry, G. and Oliver, G. (2012) 'Seeing is believing: The benefits of peer observation'. *Journal of University Learning and Teaching Practice* 9 (1). Available from <https://ro.uow.edu.au/cgi/viewcontent.cgi?referer=https://www.google.co.uk/&httpsredir=1&article=1262&context=jutlp>

Hiebert, J., Gallimore, R. and Stigler, J. (2002) 'A knowledge base for the teaching profession: What would it look like and how can we get one?' *Educational Researcher* 31 (5): 3–15.

Hiebert, J., Morris, A.K., Berk, D. and Jansen, A. (2007) 'Preparing teachers to learn from teaching'. *Journal of Teacher Education* 58 (1): 47–61.

Higher Education Academy (HEA) (2011) *The UK Professional Standards Framework for Teaching and Supporting Learning in Higher Education*. York: HEA.

Higher Education Funding Council for England (HEFCE) (2018) *Understanding and addressing differential student outcomes*. Available from <https://webarchive.nationalarchives.gov.uk/20180103171930/http://www.hefce.ac.uk/sas/inequality/differential/>

Higher Education Statistics Agency (HESA) (2017) *Destination of leavers from higher education 2015/16*. Available from <https://www.hesa.ac.uk/data-and-analysis/publications/destinations-2015-16>

Higher Education Statistics Agency (HESA) (2018) *Higher education student statistics: UK, 2016/17 – Summary*. Available from <https://www.hesa.ac.uk/news/11-01-2018/sfr247-higher-education-student-statistics>

Hinchcliffe, G. and Jolly, H. (2011) 'Graduate identity and employability'. *British Educational Research Journal* 37 (4): 563–584.

Holland, D. (2018) 'Newcastle has the highest rate of student housing in the entire country'. *Chronicle*Live, 5 September. Available from <https://www.chroniclelive.co.uk/news/north-east-news/newcastle-highest-rate-student-housing-15115702>

Holmes, L. (2013) 'Competing perspectives on graduate identity: Possession, position or process?' *Studies in Higher Education* 38 (4): 538–554.

Holmes, L. (2015) 'Becoming a graduate: The warranting of an emergent identity'. *Education and Training* 57 (2): 219–238.

Howcroft, D. (2017) 'Graduates' vocational skills for the management accountancy profession: Exploring the accounting education expectation–performance gap'. *Accounting Education* 26 (5/6): 459–481.

Hudson, P., Spooner-Lane, R. and Murray, M. (2013) 'Making mentoring explicit: Articulating pedagogical knowledge practices'. *School Leadership and Management* 33 (3): 284–301.

Iannone, P. and Simpson, A. (2017) 'University students' perceptions of summative assessment: The role of context'. *Journal of Further and Higher Education* 41 (6): 785–801.

International Center for Academic Integrity (ICAI) (2019) *Fundamental values of academic integrity*. Available from: <https://www.academicintegrity.org/fundamental-values>

Jackling, B. and De Lange, D.P. (2009) 'Do accounting graduates' skills meet the expectations of employers? A matter of convergence or divergence'. *Accounting Education* 18 (4/5): 369–385.

Jenkins, J.M. (2014) 'Pre-service teachers' observations of experienced teachers'. *Physical Educator* 71 (2): 303–319.

Joint Information Systems Committee (JISC) (2020) *The future of assessment: Five principles, five targets for 2025*. Available from <https://www.jisc.ac.uk/reports/the-future-of-assessment>

Jones, R. (2014) 'Bridging the gap: Engaging in scholarship with accountancy employers to enhance understanding of skills development and employability'. *Accounting Education* 23 (6): 527–541.

Joyner, M., Ruiz, J. and Lucia, A. (2011) 'The two-hour marathon: Who and when?' *Journal of Applied Physiology* 110 (1): 275–277.

Kennedy, H. (1997) *Learning Works: Widening Participation in Further Education*. Coventry: Further Education Funding Council.

King, A. (1993) 'From sage on the stage to guide on the side'. *College Teaching* 41 (1): 30–35.

Kirschner, P. and De Bruyckere, P. (2017) 'The myths of the digital native and the multitasker'. *Teaching and Teacher Education* 67: 135–142.

Kneale, P. (2015) *Masters Level Teaching, Learning and Assessment*. London: Palgrave Macmillan.

Knight, J. (2013) 'The changing landscape of higher education internationalisation: For better or worse?' *Perspectives: Policy and Practice in Higher Education* 17 (3): 84–90.

Knowles, M. (1984) *Andragogy in Action*. San Francisco, CA: Jossey-Bass.

Koh, K.H. (2017) *Authentic Assessment*. Oxford: Oxford Research Encyclopaedia.

Kuhn, T. (1962) *The Structure of Scientific Revolutions*. Chicago, IL: University of Chicago Press.

LaBoskey, V.K. (2004) 'The methodology of self-study and its theoretical underpinnings'. In Loughran, J.J., Hamilton, M.L., La Boskey, V.K. and Rusell, T.L., eds., *International Handbook of Self-study of Teaching and Teacher Education Practices*. Dordrecht: Kluwer Academic.

Lancaster, T. (2018) *Contract cheating*. Available from <https://thomaslancaster.co.uk/contract-cheating/>

Law, D. and Hoey, M., eds. (2018) *Perspectives on the Internationalisation of Higher Education*. Abingdon: Routledge.

Lazaric, N. (2011) 'Organizational routines and cognition: An introduction to empirical and analytical contributions'. *Journal of Institutional Economics* 7 (2): 147–156.

Leask, B. (2009) 'Using formal and informal curricula to improve interactions between home and international students'. *Journal of Studies in International Education* 13 (2): 205–221.

Ledesma, R.G. (2011) 'Academic dishonesty among undergraduate students in a Korean university'. *Research in World Economy* 2 (2). Available from <http://www.sciedu.ca/journal/index.php/rwe/article/view/490/0>

Lee, H.L., Padmanabhan, V. and Whang, S. (1997) 'Information distortion in a supply chain: The bullwhip effect'. *Management Science* 43 (4): 546–558.

Leech, E. (2014) 'Welcome to the age of Martini marketing – any time, any place, anywhere'. *The Guardian*, 21 March. Available from <https://www.theguardian.com/higher-education-network/blog/2014/mar/21/martini-marketing-higher-education>

Leinhardt, G., McCarthy Young, K. and Merriman, J. (1995) 'Integrating professional knowledge: The theory of practice and the practice of theory'. *Learning and Instruction* 5 (4): 401–408.

Lewin, K. (1947) *Field Theory in Social Science*. New York: Harper & Row.

Lewin, K. (1958) 'Group decision and social change'. In Maccoby, E.E., Newcomb, T.M. and Hartley, E.L., eds., *Readings in Social Psychology*. New York: Holt, Rinehart & Winston.

Lingfield, Lord (2012) *Professionalism in Further Education: Interim Report of the Independent Review Panel*. London: HMSO.

MacAndrew, S.B.G. and Edwards, K. (2002) 'Essays are not the only way: A case report on the benefits of authentic assessment'. *Psychology Learning and Teaching* 2 (2): 134–139.

Maguire, D. and Morris, D. (2018) *Homeward bound: Defining, understanding and aiding 'commuter students'*. HEPI Report 114. Oxford: Higher Education Policy Institute. Available from <https://www.hepi.ac.uk/wp-content/uploads/2018/12/HEPI-Home-ward-Bound-Defining-understanding-and-aiding-'commuter-students'-Report-11429_11_18Web-1.pdf>

Mallet, C.E. (1924) *A History of the University of Oxford*. London: Methuen.

Mason, G., Williams, G. and Cranmer S. (2009) 'Employability skills initiatives in higher education: What effects do they have on graduate labour market outcomes?' *Education Economics* 17 (1): 1–30.

Matheson, R., Tangney, S. and Sutcliffe, M. (2018) *Transition In, Through and Out of Higher Education*. Abingdon: Routledge.

McAleer, N. (2013) *Sir Arthur C. Clarke: Odyssey of a Visionary*. New York: Rosetta Books.

McDuff, N., Tatam, J., Beacock, O. and Ross, F. (2018) 'Closing the gap for students from black and minority ethnic backgrounds through institutional change'. *Widening Participation and Lifelong Learning* 20 (1): 79–101.

McIntyre, D. and Hagger, H. (1993) 'Teachers' expertise and models of mentoring'. In McIntyre, D., Hagger, H. and Wilkin, M. eds., *Mentoring: Perspectives on School-based Teacher Education*. London: Kogan Page.

McLuhan, M. (1962) *The Gutenberg Galaxy: The Making of Typographic Man*. Toronto: University of Toronto Press.

Mena, J., Hennissen, P. and Loughran, J. (2017) 'Developing pre-service teachers' professional knowledge of teaching: The influence of mentoring'. *Teaching and Teacher Education* 66: 47–59.

Mezirow, J. (1997) 'Transformative learning: Theory to practice'. *New Directions for Adult and Continuing Education* 74 (1): 5–12.

Moore, A. (2004) *The Good Teacher: Dominant Discourses in Teaching and Teacher Education*. Oxford: Routledge.

Mumm, K., Karm, M. and Remmik, M. (2016) 'Assessment for learning: Why assessment does not always support student teachers' learning'. *Journal of Further and Higher Education* 40 (6): 780–803.

Murray, A., Baden, D., Cashian, P., Haynes, K. and Wersun, A. (2015) *Inspirational Guide for the Implementation of PRME: UK and Ireland Edition*. Sheffield: Greenleaf Publishing.

National Union of Students (NUS) (2019a) *NUS sustainability skills survey 2018–2019*. Available from <https://sustainability.nus.org.uk/resources/nus-sustainability-skills-survey-2018-2019>

National Union of Students (NUS) (2019b) *Responsible futures: The framework*. Available from <https://sustainability.nus.org.uk/responsible-futures/about/the-criteria>

Newman, J.H. (1852) *The Idea of a University*. London: Longmans, Green.

Newton, P. (2018) 'How common is commercial contract cheating in higher education and is it increasing? A systematic review'. *Frontiers in Education* 3: 67. Available from <https://www.frontiersin.org/articles/10.3389/feduc.2018.00067/full>

Nonis, S. and Swift, C. (1998) 'Deterring cheating behavior in the marketing classroom: An analysis of the effects of demographics, attitudes, and in-class deterrent strategies'. *Journal of Marketing Education* 20 (3): 188–199.

Nutbrown, C.E. (2011) *Threads of Thinking*, 4th edition. London: Sage.

Obama, M. (2018) *Becoming*. London: Penguin Random House.

Office for National Statistics (ONS) (2019) *English indices of deprivation 2019: Mapping resources*. Available from <https://www.gov.uk/guidance/english-indices-of-deprivation-2019-mapping-resources>

Office for Standards in Education, Children's Services and Skills (Ofsted) (2019) *About us*. Available from <https://www.gov.uk/government/organisations/ofsted/about>

Office for Students (OfS) (2018) *Low higher education participation, household income and socio-economic status*. Available from <https://www.officeforstudents.org.uk/advice-and-guidance/promoting-equal-opportunities/evaluation-and-effective-practice/low-higher-education-participation-household-income-and-socio-economic-status/>

Office for Students (OfS) (2019a) *Regulatory notice 1: Access and participation plan guidance*. Available from <https://www.officeforstudents.org.uk/publications/regulatory-notice-1-access-and-participation-plan-guidance/>

Office for Students (OfS) (2019b) *Office for Students comments on latest HESA non-continuation data*. Available from <https://www.officeforstudents.org.uk/news-blog-and-events/press-and-media/office-for-students-comments-on-latest-hesa-non-continuation-data/>

Office for Students (OfS) (2019c) *Office for Students' value for money strategy 2019 to 2021*. Available from <https://www.officeforstudents.org.uk/media/336c258b-d94c-4f15-af0a-42e1be8f66a1/ofs-vfm-strategy.pdf>

Office for Students (OfS) (2019d) *The regulatory framework for higher education in England*. Available from <https://www.officeforstudents.org.uk/advice-and-guidance/regulation/the-regulatory-framework-for-higher-education-in-england/>

Office for Students (OfS) (2020) *Transforming opportunity in higher education: An analysis of 2020–21 to 2024–25 access and participation plans*. Available from <https://www.officeforstudents.org.uk/media/2efcda44-8715-4888-8d63-42c0fd6a31af/transforming-opportunity-in-higher-education.pdf>

O'Flaherty, J. and Phillips, C. (2015) 'The use of flipped classrooms in higher education: A scoping review'. *The Internet and Higher Education* 25 (October): 85–95.

Oldfield, A., Broadfoot, P., Sutherland, R. and Timms, S. (2016) Assessment in a digital age: A research review. Available from <http://www.bristol.ac.uk/media-library/sites/education/documents/researchreview.pdf>

O'Leary, M. (2012) 'Exploring the role of lesson observation in the English education system: A review of methods, models and meanings'. *Professional Development in Education* 38 (5): 791–810.

O'Leary, M. (2013) *Classroom Observation: A Guide to the Effective Observation of Teaching and Learning*. Abingdon: Routledge.

O'Leary, M., Cui, V. and French, A. (2019) *Understanding, recognising and rewarding teaching quality in higher education: An exploration of the impact and implications of the Teaching Excellence Framework*. London: University and College Union. Available from <https://www.ucu.org.uk/media/10092/Impact-of-TEF-report-Feb-2019/pdf/ImpactofTEFreportFEb2019>

Oosterheert, I. and Vermunt, J. (2001) 'Individual differences in learning to teach: Relating cognition, regulation and affect'. *Learning and Instruction* 11 (2): 133–156.

Organisation for Economic Cooperation and Development (OECD) (2019) *Education at a glance 2019: OECD indicators*. Paris: OECD Publishing. Available from <http://www.oecd.org/education/education-at-a-glance-19991487.htm/?refcode=20190209ig>

Orr, K. (2012) 'Coping, confidence and alienation: The early experience of trainee teachers in English FE'. *Journal of Education for Teaching* 38 (1): 51–65.

Osborne, D. and Plastrik, P. (1997) *Banishing Bureaucracy: The Five Strategies for Reinventing Government*. Reading, MA: Addison-Wesley.

Oser, F. and Oelkers, J. (2001) *Die Wirksamkeit der Lehrerbildungssysteme*. Zurich: Ruegger.

O'Shea, S., May, J., Stone, C. and Delahunty, J. (2017) *First-in-Family Students, University Experience and Family Life*. London: Palgrave Macmillan.

Page, D. (2019) 'The academic as consumed and consumer'. *Journal of Education Policy* (doi: 10.1080/02680939.2019.1598585).

Park, E., Park, S. and Jang, I. (2013) 'Academic cheating among nursing students'. *Nursing Education Today* 33 (1): 346–352.

Paulien, C., Meijer, A.Z. and Verloop, N. (2002) 'How can student teachers elicit experienced teachers' practical knowledge? Tools, suggestions, and significance'. *Journal of Teacher Education* 53 (5): 406–409.

Pavlov, I.P. (1927) *Conditioned Reflexes: An Investigation of the Physiological Activity of the Cerebral Cortex*. Oxford: Oxford University Press.

Peake, G. (2006) *Observation of the practice of teaching: Research findings from the University of Huddersfield Consortium for PCET*. Available from <http://escalate.ac.uk/3060>

Perkins, H. (1990) *The Rise of Professional Society*. London: Routledge.

Piaget, J. (1952) *The Origins of Intelligence in Children*. New York: International Universities Press.

Pinar, M. and Unlu, E. (2020) 'Evaluating the potential effect of the increased importance of the impact component in the Research Excellence Framework'. *British Educational Research Journal* 46 (1): 140–160.

Podmore, V. (2012) *Observation: Origins and Approaches*. Oxford: Oxford University Press.

Porter, M.E. (1979) 'How competitive forces shape strategy', *Harvard Business Review* 57 (2), March/April: 137–145.

Porter, M.E. (2008) *The Five Competitive Forces that Shape Strategy: An interview with Michael E. Porter* (video). Harvard Business Publishing. Available from <https://hbr.org/video/2226587624001/the-five-competitive-forces-that-shape-strategy>

Powell, A. (2020) *People with disabilities in employment*. Briefing Paper 7540, 3 January. London: House of Commons. Available from <https://commonslibrary.parliament.uk/research-briefings/cbp-7540/>

Power, A. and Holland, L. (2018) 'Are students empty vessels or can previous experience enhance future practice?' *British Journal of Midwifery* 28 (2). Available from <https://www.magonlinelibrary.com/doi/abs/10.12968/bjom.2018.26.2.125?af=R&>

Prensky, M. (2001) 'Digital natives, digital immigrants'. *On the Horizon* 9 (5). Available from <https://www.marcprensky.com/writing/Prensky%20-%20Digital%20Natives,%20Digital%20Immigrants%20-%20Part1.pdf>

Pressick-Kilborn, K. and te Riele, K. (2008) 'Learning from reciprocal peer observation: A collaborative self-study'. *Studying Teacher Education* 4 (1): 61–75.

Prince, M. (2004) 'Does active learning work? A review of the research'. *Journal of Engineering Education* 93 (3): 223–231.

Principles for Responsible Management Education (PRME) (2012) *Inspirational Guide for the Implementation of PRME: Placing sustainability at the heart of management education*. Leeds: GSE Research. Available from <https://www.sustainabilityexchange.ac.uk/files/prmeinspirationalguide1stedition2012.pdf>

Principles for Responsible Management Education (PRME) (2013) *Inspirational Guide for the Implementation of PRME:* 2nd edition, *Learning to go beyond.* Sheffield: Greenleaf Publishing.

Quality Assurance Agency (QAA) (2019) *What we do.* Available from <https://www.qaa.ac.uk/en/about-us/what-we-do>

Quintos, M.A.M. (2017) 'A study on the prevalence and correlates of academic dishonesty in four undergraduate degree programmes'. *Asia Pacific Journal of Multidisciplinary Research* 5 (1): 135–154.

Race, P. (2014) *Making Learning Happen: A Guide for Post-Compulsory Education.* London: Sage.

RARA (2020) *Raising awareness, raising aspirations: A targeted personal tutoring support programme.* Available from <http://www.raratutor.ac.uk>

Rawson, K., Dunlosky, J. and Sciartelli, S. (2013) 'The power of successive relearning: Improving performance on course exams and long term retention'. *Educational Psychology Review* 25 (4): 523–548.

Reay, D., Crozier, G. and Clayton, J. (2010) '"Fitting in" or "standing out": Working class students in UK higher education'. *British Educational Research Journal* 36 (1): 107–124.

Reilly, D., Sun, W., Vellam, I. and Warren, L. (2019) 'Improving the attainment gap of direct entry Chinese students: Lessons learnt and recommendations'. *Compass: Journal of Learning and Teaching* 12 (1). Available from <https://journals.gre.ac.uk/index.php/compass/article/view/932>

Rich, J. (2015) *Why TEF must measure employability not employment.* Available from <https://wonkhe.com/blogs/employability-johnsons-tef>

Richards, J.C. and Farrell, T.S.C. (2011) 'Classroom observation in teaching practice'. In *Practice Teaching: A Reflective Approach.* Cambridge: Cambridge University Press.

Robinson, K. (2010) *Changing Education Paradigms,* RSA Animate Series. Available from <https://www.thersa.org/discover/publications-and-articles/rsa-comment/2010/10/rsa-animate—changing-education-paradigms>

Rogers, E. (1962) *Diffusion of Innovations.* New York: Free Press of Glencoe.

Roig, M. (2001) 'Plagiarism and paraphrasing criteria of college and university professors'. *Ethics and Behavior* 11 (3): 307–323.

Roxa, T. and Martensson, K. (2009) 'Significant conversations and significant networks – exploring the backstage of the teaching arena'. *Studies in Higher Education* 34 (5): 547–559.

Roxa, T., Martensson, K. and Alveteg, M. (2011) 'Understanding and influencing teaching and learning cultures at university: A network approach'. *Higher Education* 62 (1): 99–111.

Ryan, A. and Tilbury, D. (2013) *Flexible pedagogies: New pedagogical ideas.* York: The Higher Education Academy. Available from <https://www.advance-he.ac.uk/knowledge-hub/flexible-pedagogies-new-pedagogical-ideas>

Sachs, J. (2005) 'Teacher education and the development of professional identity: Learning to be a teacher'. In Denicolo, P.M. and Kompf, M., eds., *Connecting Policy and Practice: Challenges for Teaching and Learning in Schools and Universities.* London: Routledge.

Sambell, K., McDowell, L. and Montgomery, C. (2013) *Assessment for Learning in Higher Education.* Abingdon: Routledge.

San Pedro, M. (2012) 'Feedback and feedforward: Focal points for improving academic performance'. *Journal of Technology and Science Education* 2 (2): 77–85.

Schön, D.A. (1983) *The Reflective Practitioner: How Professionals Think in Action.* New York: Basic Books.

Schön, D.A. (2009) *Educating the Reflective Practitioner: Towards a New Design for Teaching and Learning in the Professions*. London: Jossey-Bass.

Schultz, T.W. (1971) *Investment in Human Capital: The Role of Education and of Research*. London: Collier-Macmillan.

Scudamore, R. (2013) *Engaging home and international students: A guide for new lecturers*. York: The Higher Education Academy. Available from <https://www.advance-he. ac.uk/knowledge-hub/engaging-home-and-international-students-guide-new-lecturers>

Sellars, M. (2017) *Reflective Practice for Teachers*, 2nd edition. Los Angeles, CA: Sage.

Selwyn, N. (2014) *Distrusting Educational Technology: Critical Questions for Changing Times*. Abingdon: Routledge

Sharples, M. (2019) *Practical Pedagogy: 40 New Ways to Teach and Learn*. Abingdon: Routledge.

Shattock, M. (2006) 'Policy drivers in UK higher education in historical perspective: "Inside out", "outside in" and the contribution of research'. *Higher Education Quarterly* 60 (2): 130–140.

Simmons, R. (2008) 'Golden years? Further education colleges under local authority control'. *Journal of Further and Higher Education* 32(4): 359–371.

Sjølie, E. (2014) 'The role of theory in teacher education: Reconsidered from a student teacher perspective'. *Journal of Curriculum Studies* 46 (6): 729–750.

Smetherham, C. (2006) 'First among equals? Evidence on the contemporary relationship between educational credentials and the occupational structure'. *Journal of Education and Work* 19 (1): 29–45.

Smith, C.V. and Cardaciotto, L. (2011) 'Is active learning like broccoli? Student perceptions of active learning in large lecture classes'. *Journal of the Scholarship of Teaching and Learning* 11 (1): 53–61.

Smith, J.D.N. (2005) 'Understanding the beliefs, concerns and priorities of trainee teachers: A multi disciplinary approach'. *Mentoring and Tutoring: Partnership in Learning* 13 (2): 205–219.

Smith, T.R., Langenbacher, M., Kudlac, C. and Fera, A.G. (2013) 'Deviant reactions to the college pressure cooker: A test of general strain theory on undergraduate students in the United States'. *International Journal of Criminal Justices Sciences* 8 (2): 88–104.

Social Mobility Commission (SMC) (2019) *State of the Nation 2018–19: Social Mobility in Great Britain*. London: SMC. Available from <https://assets.publishing.service. gov.uk/government/uploads/system/uploads/attachment_data/file/798404/SMC_ State_of_the_Nation_Report_2018-19.pdf>

Stevenson, J. and Clegg, S. (2011) 'Possible selves: Students orienting themselves towards the future through extracurricular activity'. *British Educational Research Journal* 37 (2): 231–246.

Strevens, P. (1974) 'Some basic principles of teacher training'. *English Language Teaching Journal* 29 (1): 19–27.

Struyven, K., Dochy, F. and Janssens, S. (2005) 'Students' perceptions about evaluation and assessment in higher education: A review'. *Assessment and Evaluation in Higher Education* 30 (4): 325–341.

Swaffield, S. (2011) 'Getting to the heart of authentic assessment for learning'. *Assessment in Education: Principles, Policy and Practice* 18 (4): 433–449.

Swan, J. (1993) 'Metaphor in action: The observation schedule in a reflective approach to teacher education', *ELT Journal* 47 (3): 242–249.

Taylor, B. (2018) 'What breaking the 4-minute mile taught us about the limits of conventional thinking'. *Harvard Business Review*, 9 March. Available from <https://hbr. org/2018/03/what-breaking-the-4-minute-mile-taught-us-about-the-limits-of-conventional-thinking>

Tenenberg, J. (2014) 'Learning through observing peers in practice'. *Studies in Higher Education* 41 (4), 1–18.

TESTA (2015) *Transforming the Experience of Students Through Assessment*. Available from <https://www.testa.ac.uk/index.php>

The Brilliant Club (2020) *About us*. Available from <https://thebrilliantclub.org/about-the-brilliant-club/what-is-tbc/>

Thomas, L. and Jones, R. (2017) *Student engagement in the context of commuter students*. London: The Student Engagement Partnership. Available from <https://www.lizthomasassociates.co.uk/projects/2018/Commuter%20student%20engagement.pdf>

Thompson, C. and Wolstencroft, P. (2018) 'Trust into mistrust: The uncertain marriage between public and private sector practice for middle managers in education'. *Research in Post-Compulsory Education* 23 (2): 213–230.

Thomson, K., Bell, A. and Hendry, G. (2015) 'Peer observation of teaching: The case for learning just by watching'. *Higher Education Research and Development* 34 (5): 1060–1062.

Tomlinson, M. (2017) 'Student perceptions of themselves as "consumers" of higher education'. *British Journal of Sociology of Education* 38 (4): 450–467.

Turner, I.J. (2014) 'Lecture theatre pantomime: A creative delivery approach for teaching undergraduate transcription and translation'. *Innovative Practice in Higher Education* 2 (1): 1–13.

UNICEF (2018) *An unfair start: Inequality in children's education in rich countries*, Innocenti Report Card 15. Florence: UNICEF Office of Research – Innocenti.

United Nations (UN) (2020) *The SDG Accord*. Available from <https://www.sdgaccord.org>

Universities and Colleges Admissions Service (UCAS) (2016) *Through the lens of students: How perceptions of higher education influence applicants' choices*. Available from <https://www.ucas.com/sites/default/files/through-the-lens-of-students.pdf>

Universities and Colleges Admissions Service (UCAS) (2017) *Contextualised admissions and what it means for your students*. Available from <https://www.ucas.com/advisers/guides-and-resources/adviser-news/news/contextualised-admissions-and-what-it-means-your-students>

Universities UK (UUK) (2019a) *International facts and figures 2019*. Available from <https://www.universitiesuk.ac.uk/International/Documents/2019/International%20facts%20and%20figures%20slides.pdf>

Universities UK (UUK) (2019b) *Black, Asian and Minority Ethnic student attainment at UK universities: #Closingthegap*. Available from <https://www.universitiesuk.ac.uk/policy-and-analysis/reports/Documents/2019/bame-student-attainment-uk-universities-closing-the-gap.pdf>

University and College Union (UCU) (2017) *UCU workload survey 2016*. Available from <https://www.ucu.org.uk/media/8196/Executive-summary---Workload-is-an-education-issue-UCU-workload-survey-report-2016/pdf/ucu_workloadsurvey_summary_jun16.pdf>

UPP Foundation (2019) *Leading universities pledge commitment to local communities*. Available from <https://upp-foundation.org/leading-universities-pledge-commitment-to-local-communities/>

Villarroel, V., Boud, D., Bloxham, S., Bruna, D. and Bruna, C. (2019) 'Using principles of authentic assessment to redesign written examinations and tests'. *Innovations in Education and Teaching International* 57 (1): 38–49.

Vygotsky, L. (1978) *Mind in Society: The Development of Higher Psychological Processes*. Cambridge, MA: Harvard University Press.

Wadsworth, B.J. (2004) *Piaget's Theory of Cognitive and Affective Development: Foundations of Constructivism*. London: Longman.

Walker, R., Jenkins, M. and Voce, J. (2017) 'The rhetoric and reality of technology-enhanced learning developments in UK higher education: Reflections on recent UCISA research findings'. *Interactive Learning Environments* 26 (7): 858–868.

Warren, L. and Reilly, D. (2019) *Addressing the attainment gap: Business schools can lead the way by providing an inclusive approach to the student experience*. Available from <https://charteredabs.org/addressing-the-attainment-gap-business-schools-can-lead-the-way-by-providing-an-inclusive-approach-to-the-student-experience/>

Werbach, K. (2014) '(Re)defining gamification: A process approach'. In Spagnolli, A., Chittaro. L. and Gamberini, L., eds., *Persuasive Technology: 9th International Conference, PERSUASIVE 2014*, 266-272. Cham: Springer.

Whitley, B.E. (1998) 'Factors associated with cheating among college students: A review'. *Research in Higher Education* 39: 235–274.

Wihlborg, M. and Robson, S. (2018) 'Internationalisation of higher education: Drivers, rationales, priorities, values and impacts'. *European Journal of Higher Education* 8 (1): 8–18.

Wilcox, P., Winn, S. and Fyvie-Gauld, M. (2012) 'It was nothing to do with the university, it was just the people': The role of social support in the first year experience of higher education'. *Studies in Higher Education* 30 (6): 707–722.

Wilde, O. (1890) *The Picture of Dorian Gray*. Brooklyn: Millennium Publications.

Wolstencroft, P. and de Main, L. (2020) 'Why didn't you tell me that before? Engaging undergraduate students in feedback and feedforward within UK higher education'. *Journal of Further and Higher Education* (doi: 10.1080/0309877X.2020.1759517).

Woodall, T., Hiller, A. and Resnick, S. (2014) 'Making sense of higher education: Students as consumers and the value of the university experience'. *Studies in Higher Education* 39 (1): 48–67.

World Health Organisation (WHO) (2020) *WHO Director-General's opening remarks at the media briefing on COVID-19 – 11 March 2020*. Available from <https://www.who.int/dg/speeches/detail/who-director-general-s-opening-remarks-at-the-media-briefing-on-covid-19---11-march-2020>

Wragg, E.C. (2011) *An Introduction to Classroom Observation*, 2nd edition. London: Routledge.

Yorke, M. (2004) 'Employability in the undergraduate curriculum: Some student perspectives'. *European Journal of Education* 39 (4): 409–427.

Zeichner, H. (2010) 'Rethinking the connections between campus courses and field experiences in college- and university-based teacher education'. *Journal of Education* 61 (1/2): 89–99.

Zhou, X. and Orim, S.M. (2015) 'Impact investigation of using a digital literacy technology on a Module: Case study of Tophat'. *International Journal of Learning, Teaching and Educational Research* 11 (1): 99–116.

Zhou, X. and Wolstencroft, P. (2020) *Digital masters? Reflecting on the readiness of students and staff for digital learning*. Available from <https://www.bera.ac.uk/blog/digital-masters-reflecting-on-the-readiness-of-students-and-staff-for-digital-learning>

Zulaikha, M., Valcke, M. and De Wever, B. (2017) 'Are they ready to teach? Student teachers' readiness for the job with reference to teacher competence frameworks'. *Journal of Education for Teaching* 43 (2): 151–170.

Index

Printed in Great Britain
by Amazon

49560639R00106